the TRUE YOU *in* YOU

The Discovery of Your True Identity

Moïse Kabongo

Foreword by Dr. Myles Munroe

This book is lovingly dedicated to:

Mike (Moïse Jr.), Elisha and Myles Moïse Kabongo:

My beloved sons and my beloved daughter, who make me live up to the fatherhood image of God. The discovery of yourself makes you natural and an original, not a fabricated imitation. You guys have something that this world needs.

ACKNOWLEDGMENTS

No achievement in life is without the help of many known and unknown individuals who have contributed to our lives. We are all the sum total of what we have learned from others, and we owe any measure of success to the array of input from so many. Here are just a few who made this work possible:

- To my earthly father and my first mentor, Sr. Moïse Kabongo who planted in me the foundation for a spiritual life according to the Bible. You taught me to love Jesus and worship Him in spirit.

- To my mother, Julienne Kabongo who taught me to be a man of virtue.

- To all my 10 sisters and my brother.

- To Dr. Myles and mama Ruth Munroe: You have been an example of success and outstanding leaders in my life. In the same way that Paul encouraged the Corinthians to imitate him despite their thousands of instructors in Christ (1 Corinthians 4: 15–16), Dr. Myles, you became my mentor and teacher in the leadership of wisdom of the Kingdom. Your sudden death gave me even more courage to teach the kingdom of God. You have so impacted my life that one of my sons is called "Myles"

- To you pastor Matthew and Deborah Adeyemo, my parents in the faith. Your spiritual rigor is an education and challenge in my spiritual journey.

- To KIIC Citizens all over the world, I thank you for your support and love. You have trusted me in this big vision that God has given me.

- To the Father of our Lord Jesus Christ, the Creator and the provider of all things, Elohim.

I have had the opportunity to meet Pastor Moïse Kabongo at several leadership meetings with Dr. Myles Munroe in Nassau, Bahamas. I thank God for introducing him to me through my good friend, Marlise Heller. Pastor Kabongo is one who is constantly expanding, developing and training his mind which, I believe, qualifies him to write this book. I am amazed by the substance, values and purity found in this literature. I believe that everyone who is seriously interested in expanding their mind, discovering themselves and wishing to live effectively as Kingdom citizens here on earth, should take the journey into the pages of this life-changing work.

The content of Pastor Kabongo's book will revolutionize your thoughts; provoke the leader to arise from the ashes of hopelessness, and force the real you to truly live life in a challenging world. I commend my friend and co-labourer in the Lord, Pastor Kabongo, for a work that is much needed in these testing times. I encourage each reader to take the journey into greatness and self-discovery, and embrace the gift that has been poured out to us in the pages of this great book.

Pepe Ramnath, PhD
Research Scientist/Microscopist, Author & Pastor

CONTENTS

by Dr. Myles Munroe

The human struggle for purpose and meaning is the common driving force for all human behavior. This same struggle reduces all men from every nation, race, gender and socio-economic status to the same basic need. Who are we? Where did we come from? Why are we here? What can we do? Where are we going? These are all questions that fill the collective human heart and mind? These questions are also known to be the source of human frustration and their answers are the age-old pursuit of every generation of men throughout the ages.

Philosophers, spiritual sages, prophets, psychologists and natural scientists have all attempted to find the answers to these uncomfortable questions and the search goes on today.

I, too, have traveled that 'road of human search' and could say, without hesitation, that I have found the answers to the questions that produce the peace, fulfillment and personal satisfaction for which we are all searching. Where did I find these answers? In the message and life of the young Jewish Rabbi who 2000 years ago announced the arrival of the mysterious 'Kingdom of God' on earth. Jesus Christ and his life-changing message of the Kingdom of Heaven and its unique culture, economy, values, morals and laws showed the superior nature of this heavenly government. When I understood the essence of his concepts and practical component to contemporary life, the answers to all of my questions fell into place.

Moïse Kabongo's exceptional work presents these concepts and this message in such a profound, yet simple, way. In his unique, yet exciting, approach to the subject, the author leaps over complicated theological jargon and presents us with a reader-friendly understanding of the principles and purposes of God for every human on earth. His background as a trained Catholic Priest gives him a special perspective of religion and its contrasting comparison with the Kingdom message serving up insights and revelations that takes on a journey to discovering the original purpose and plan of God for mankind.

I challenge you to read every page and peal the treasure of knowledge, understanding and wisdom buried in every sentence. Watch your life change, as mine did when I read his manuscript. This book is destined to become a classic, and will serve many generations to come as a guiding light to God's Original Plan and His purposes for you and your fellow planet dwellers.

Dr. Myles E. Munroe
BFM International,
Nassau Bahamas

like one of the Kingdom Quotes of my father in faith Dr. Myles Munroe:

'What are you thinking?' He quotes: 'Until you know the truth about you, you are living a lie. I do not trust anybody to tell me the truth about me because the truth about me, nobody really knows.'

The Bible states:

> *'Eye hath not seen, nor ear heard, neither have entered into the heart of man, the things which God hath prepared for them that love him. But God hath revealed them unto us by his spirit.'*

> (1 Corinthians 2:9–10)

That is why we have to get information from the Truth. Jesus said that; *'You shall know the truth and the truth will make you free'* (John 8:31). It will make you free from people's opinions. Until you get the truth from the Holy Spirit, you have been living a lie.

The Bible shows us:

> *'The World cannot accept Him, because it neither sees Him nor knows Him.'*

(John 14:7)

The Holy Spirit tells you who you are, and the world says, 'We disagree.' The Holy Spirit says what you can accomplish, and the world says, 'That is not true.' Also you need to know that when the truth really hits you, half of your family most likely will disagree with you because the truth about you is so unnatural to them.

Paul says:

> *'The world cannot judge you when you are walking in the Spirit of truth.'*

(1 Corinthians 2:15)

The Holy Spirit knows the truth about you, but the world cannot judge you. People cannot discern or understand it, which means when the Lord reveals to you what is true about you; many of the people in your immediate world will not be able to handle it.

People still look at me and say, 'That little boy from Congo-Kinshasa, who does he think he is?' I am glad that they don't know who I think I am. It is better to have your own thoughts about yourself, and not allow anyone to 'think' for you.

You can tell that some people do not like you in the first place, so you know that they are not going to think well of you anyhow. Some people are longing for you to fail. Do not look for 'failure seekers' for any encouragement. The world may not be able to receive the information that the Holy Spirit has about you.

The world does not even know who the citizens of God's kingdom are; and the world cannot even see the Holy Spirit.

When a person's goal overpowers him and he decides to 'conform' to society's ideals—he loses his original attitude in order to adopt the one his environment imposes on him. In other words, man's thoughts can be reworked by the system of this world. We all know that there is nothing more powerful than attitude. Our attitude is the manifestation of who we think we are. We live our lives according to who we think we are. And the oppression that man deliberately creates without prior knowledge that it will harm him, attacks his thoughts and changes his true self. So without realizing it, man accepts and lives by the identity, which his environment has fashioned for him. Man denies himself in order to adopt or copy the 'becoming' already established by the system.

The Roman Empire was the most powerful in the history of the world, and remains so today. No government has ruled and dominated the entire world as the Roman Empire did. It was in this context of oppression that the greatest man ever came into the world. His name was Jesus. He came under Roman oppression to tell man to live life as his true self and not accept what is forced upon him by oppression. The Romans believed they were a superior race. They claimed that anyone who was not Roman was inferior, inhuman. They even found a theology to justify their beliefs. The Roman Empire was built on a pagan religion which originated in Greek philosophy, and the Greeks preached the inferiority and superiority of races. The Romans adopted this Greek philosophy.

There are 6.7 billion people on Earth and 4.7 billion of them live in what we call the Third World. The Third World consists only of nations who have not had the opportunity to take part in the Industrial Revolution. And there is not a Third World location; but it is about the mentality. And the people of most of these countries have been used by industry as human machines. The majority of people on Earth, therefore, are still struggling to rid themselves of the damage caused by oppression. Africa, South America and the East are examples of this. This explains why only a quarter of the world's population lives in freedom. The Romans became experts in oppression. In fact, Europe is the Roman Empire disintegrated. This is how Europe adopted Roman philosophy. It is why in most of the colonies the same concept exists where the oppressor automatically considers himself to be superior to the oppressed.

On studying almost all the theories on the origins of man, I rediscovered one single truth which is that of the existence of God who created man in his image and likeness. This is a truth which can only be accepted and experienced by faith in the Lord Jesus Christ. This truth is confirmed and authenticated by the coming of Jesus Christ to Earth and by his resurrection from death. This is a truth that no man can disprove because almost all the other theories are based only on man's reasoning. Well, man's reasoning is limited. And the Lord Jesus Christ is above human reasoning. He is in fact both the master and the source of it.

So, I posed myself these questions:

- Who am I?

- Is my current life the one given to me by my creator?

- Why was I born?

- Was I created to suffer?

- Do I live as my real self?

It is these questions that this book seeks to answer and the key to success in life is discovering your uniqueness and significance. Sit back and enjoy the journey of your discovery!

'THE ONLY THING THAT CAN
REALLY STOP YOU FROM LIVING
YOUR DREAM IS YOU.'

CHAPTER 1

RELIGION AND MAN-MADE GOVERNMENT SYSTEMS ARE NOT THE ANSWER

The year 2000 was a year of excitement. As an IT Consultant in Germany, I remember how concerned we were about our Information Technology Systems at the time. The big IT industries predicted a system crash—a system failure while we were passing from the year 1999 to 2000, and banks were looking for the best strategies to prevent chaos. How great was our joy when all systems responded correctly!

However, the terrorist attacks of September 11th, 2001 changed everything. At that time, I had begun to ask myself how a man was capable of killing in the name of a particular religion. I was so disappointed that I started to search for answers by studying religions.

During my Catholic priest training, I studied different religions and concepts. I did not know, however, that religion is unable to provide all answers or every solution to the problems of mankind or the world. Nonetheless, religion is capable in some ways of being responsible for various problems. Religion has involved killing since the beginning—when I think about Catholic crusades, Islamic conquests, wars related to the Protestant Reformation...I ask myself again what religion really is. The next paragraph is an attempt to define religion.

The definition of the word 'religion' is ambiguous. This commonly used word seems to have achieved ambiguity or uncertainty in modern times, apparently a reflection of the multi-ethnic and philosophically diverse global culture in which we currently find ourselves. Even many spiritual leaders would admit religion is a difficult word to define. The English word 'religion' is derived from the Middle English 'religioun' which came from the old French 'religion'. It may originally have been derived from the Latin word 'religo' which means 'good Faith', 'ritual', and other similar definitions. Or it may have come from the Latin 'religäre' which means 'to tie fast'. Defining the word 'religion' is fraught with difficulty. Many attempts have been made and debate has ensued forever as to whose interpretations may be correct and whose may not be.

Dictionary definitions:

> *Barnes & Noble (Cambridge) Encyclopedia* (1990):

> '...no single definition will suffice to encompass the varied sets of traditions, practices, and ideas which constitute different religions.'

The Concise Oxford Dictionary (1990):

'Human recognition of superhuman controlling power and especially of a personal God entitled to obedience.'

This definition would not consider some Buddhist sects as religions and many Unitarian Universalists are excluded by this description. Strictly interpreted, it would also reject polytheistic religions, since it refers to 'a' personal God.

Merriam Webster's Online Dictionary:

'A cause, principle, or system of beliefs held to with ardor and faith.'

This is a curious definition because it does not require elements often associated with religion, such as deity, morality, worldview, etc. Also it requires that a person pursue their religion with enthusiasm. Many people identify themselves with a specific religion, but are not intensely engaged with their faith.

Webster's New World Dictionary (Third College Edition):

'Any specific system of belief and worship, often involving a code of ethics and a philosophy.'

This definition would exclude religions that do not engage in worship. It implies that there are two important components to religion:

'One's belief in and worship of a deity or deities'.

'One's ethical behavior towards other persons'.

This dual nature of religion is expressed clearly in the Christian Scriptures (New Testament) in Matthew 22:36–39:

> *'"Teacher, what is the great commandment in the law?" Jesus said unto him, "Thou shall love the Lord thy God with all thy heart, and with all thy soul, and with all thy mind. This is the first and great commandment. And the second is like unto it, Thou shall love thy neighbor as thyself."'*

Qumran Bet 'A Community Striving to Come to the Pure Essence of the Worship of YHWH,' cites definitions from an unknown dictionary:

- religion (ri-lij'[uh] n) n.

- The beliefs, attitudes, emotions, behavior, etc., man's relationship with the powers and principles of the universe, especially with a deity or deities; also, any particular system of such beliefs, attitudes, etc.

- An essential part or a practical test of the spiritual life.

- An object of conscientious devotion or scrupulous care: e.g. His work is a religion to him.

- Obs. Religious practice or belief.'

The Christian Apologetics & Research Ministry (CARM):

> 'An organized system of belief that generally seeks to understand purpose, meaning, goals and methods of spiritual things. These spiritual things can be God, people in relation to God, salvation, after life, purpose of life, order of the cosmos, etc.'

Dr. Myles Munroe in his 'Kingdom's Teachings' defines religion as:

> 'The worship of a deity through a set of beliefs expressed through set rituals, customs and rites producing a sectarian distinction and group.'

This difficulty of defining religion is a sign that religion fails as an answer to man's problems. The study shows clearly that every major problem in history and in our contemporary world can be traced back to some religious foundation. The Crusades, the Inquisition, wars related to the Protestant Reformation and the Catholic counter-reformation, slavery, ethnic cleansing, apartheid, segregation, racial discrimination and the New York terrorist attacks are evidence that religion is not the answer to man's problem but the cause, the bondage and the confusion. All these acts of cruelty have been justified by some religious code or system. Therefore, many millions have turned away from forms of institutionalized religions and opted to embrace such philosophies as humanism, communism and spiritualism. And some have simply given up and lost all hope in humanity. Religion is supposed to provide the solution to mankind's problems and bring hope and faith for life. Instead it seems to some to have created more problems throughout history than it has solved.

We find that religion exists in some form in every human culture, in primitive and modern human societies. This ambiguity raises some questions:

- What is the source of religion?

- Why is man in search of a supernatural realm?

Dr. Myles Munroe, in his book 'Kingdom Principles', answers these questions with the conclusion that religion is the result of an inherent hunger in the human spirit that man cannot define yet must seek to satisfy. This indefinable hunger, arising from a vacuum created by the loss of something man used to possess, drives him to pursue answers beyond his own realm. Man is looking for the power to control the circumstances of his daily life. All of us look for meaning for our existence and the power to determine the future and predict the unknown; power over death and life. Man is like a machine or a car that has lost control and does not know where to start or where to go. He is looking for security in religion, politics, money, fame, notoriety, recognition or influence.

What is this 'something' that man used to possess and later lost?

We must first find and understand the origin of man to answer this question. The first book of Moses (Genesis: Chap 1 v 26) tells us clearly the origin of man and why he was created:

> *'26. And God said; Let us make man in our image, after our likeness: and let them have dominion over the fish of the sea and over the fowl of the air, and over the cattle, and over all the earth, and over every creeping thing that creeps upon the earth'. (KJV)*

In this statement, we find the nature, the purpose and the mandate behind mankind's creation. Three words in this passage that are very important, significant and have a deep essence of man are: 'image', 'likeness' and 'dominion'.

The original Hebrew word for image is 'Tselem'—meaning nature. The Hebrew word for likeness is 'Demuth', which signifies the original after which a thing is patterned. Those words define and describe our design, capacity, potential and purpose as human beings made to reflect the personhood of our Creator. In others words, God created man to act and function like Him. The Hebrew word for dominion is 'Mamlakah', which can be translated as 'kingdom', 'sovereign rule' or 'royal power', 'government', 'influence', 'management', 'control', 'authority'...

In essence, mankind was created to have God's nature and God's character, to function like God and to have rulership over the earth. Therefore, man is a leader to whom God gave the mandate to carry out His will on earth. The dominion that God empowered within man is the foundation and source of his need to control and rule or govern his environment and circumstances. This Kingdom mandate validates man's desire for power. Power is natural to the human spirit.

What did man do to lose this power; to lose his original design? Mankind disobeyed his Creator (through Adam and Eve's rebellion) and he lost his dominion over the earth. He lost the mandate for his kingdom, his gift of divine power. And thank God, who so loves mankind that He created and sent His son Jesus Christ to earth to re-establish His number one priority: to extend His Heavenly Kingdom on earth through mankind. The control of the earth is this thing that man lost. Therefore, man developed his own culture which is not based on God's purposes and principles.

Does anyone doubt that the leaders of this world are relentlessly removing God's laws and His ways as the reference point for our national and personal way of life? Man created religion and all the spiritual concepts that we have today. In many ways, religion is a source of oppression because it is often built on traditions and belief systems that do not allow the follower to think for themselves or to question those standards or traditions. In many ways religion is also used to minimize thinking. From the Leninist perspective religion seems to have a paralytic effect on people in that it doesn't allow them to be progressive in their thinking or expansive in their views or to be developmental in their perspective of life.

When you carefully study the Bible and all manmade religions, you will conclude that there is a distinct difference between religion and the Kingdom of God. Jesus' message and His work were part of a practical, need—meeting, life-transforming philosophy. We, therefore, need to revisit and rediscover the Jesus of the four Gospels and the message He taught, and compare that to the religion called Christianity that we have developed. We need to know that the Bible does not talk about religion but it talks about a King, His son and His Kingdom. The Bible is not about religion.

Jesus restored man to his original design. He came to recolonize the earth. The bible shows us that God planned to redeem and restore mankind from the beginning of creation. Adam and Eve failed at the beginning of creation. But God was not discouraged; He maintained His redemption through Jesus. To restore God's purpose, Jesus came as a representative of the legal authority of the earth: man. He came as a human being, the second Adam, the second beginning of a new family of men who would be devoted to God. Jesus, the second person of the Trinity voluntarily put aside His Heavenly Glory and came to earth as a man.

Philippians 2:6–8:

> *'Who, being in the form of God, thought it not robbery to be equal with God: But made himself of no reputation, and took upon him the form of a servant, and was made in the likeness of men: And being found in fashion as a man, he humbled himself, and became obedient unto death, even death on the cross'.*

Coming as a man gave Jesus the legal right to reclaim humanity and the earth for God. To restore man's broken relationship with God, it was necessary for Jesus to live a sinless life and to choose to do God's Will. Only a perfectly righteous man who desired to do God's Will could redeem humanity.

1 John 3: 8 tells clearly the reason why Jesus came to earth:

> *'He that committeth sin is of the devil; for the devil sinneth from the beginning. For this purpose, the Son of God was manifested, that he might destroy the works of the devil'. (KJV)*

Satan became the god of this world when he successfully tempted Adam and Eve to reject God's ways. (Genesis 3:1–24). Yet Christ delivered us from Satan's dominion. Even though we live in a fallen world, we do not belong to it, but to God's kingdom. Satan no longer has authority over us; rather, we have authority over him in the name of Jesus.

Colossians 1:13:

> *'Who hath delivered us from the power of darkness, and hath translated [us] into the kingdom of his dear Son', (KJV)*

I understand that I have been created in the image-likeness of God and the first thing that God gave to man is dominion (Kingdom, government, power...). I am a special creation of God. He did not create the rest of His creatures in His image; only man. What a privilege! What a benefit! What an advantage that God has given to man. The principle of procreation shows us that a dog gives birth to a puppy a chicken gives birth to a chick...and God created a man in His nature.

Man has God's nature. Man's source is God despite what science with its limitations can say. Man came out of God. This statement is too big for Christianity. Religion does not like such a statement because it likes to see man living in ignorance, in dependence, in bondage and then it can control him. Nevertheless, this is the truth written for us in the Bible.

My learning this truth about man and the discovery of what man *truly* is actually changed my life. My intention on writing "The True You in You" is so that through studying this book, you too will achieve a life that is changed. Another goal of mine of course is that you become what God made you to be and not what mankind wants you to be.

I have good news for all who have given up or turned to institutionalized forms of religion. Jesus came on earth for everyone, including them, and He restored them to their original status of being. Jesus came to tell us about the Kingdom in which we should live.

The time has come for everyone to discover the true message of Jesus in the Bible. This Kingdom is the answer to mankind's greatest need and offers a solution to this universal human search. Ninety percent of all the national and international problems facing our world today have their origins in government or religion. The life of Christ is the energizing force that transforms and heals that which is broken. Religious dogma or mysticism does not change lives.

'EVERYONE IS BORN UNIQUE BUT MOST OF US DIE COPIES. LEARN WHO YOU ARE AND WORK ON BRINGING YOUR TRUE SELF OUT.'

CHAPTER 2

QUESTIONS OF THE HUMAN HEART

Every human being is on the road of search. We search, without knowing, to answer these five questions because their answers produce peace, fulfillment and satisfaction.

These questions control everything we do. They control our environment, our economy, our family... and they even cause the destruction of the family. These five questions control why young people join gangs, why young people will fight to steal designer clothes...they are powerful questions. The same questions control the poor and the rich. These questions are the questions to which *you* need answers in order to live a full life.

Who am I? The average person in the world has not answered that question. 99% of people on the earth have not answered this question. People do not deal with this question because it is a question of identity. The question '*Who am I?*' is a frustrating question because society does not allow you to explore it. Our culture does not allow you to be yourself, to discover who you are. The world wants to make you who *it* wants you to be. And if you attempt to move away from that, you become an irritation to society. This question is critical.

Ninety percent of the people in the world are suffering from an identity crisis. That is why we wear designer clothes. We wear Calvin Klein and Nike because we do not have a value for our own self. Some people think that if they do not wear something of identity they have no worth.

Where am I from? That question seems very simple but it is not. Because when you ask someone where he is from he may tell you he comes from Africa or from the States...that question has nothing to do with your ethnic background. '*Where am I from?*' is a very strategic question. The average person never answers this question. It is a question of heritage. When I ask a white man where he is from, he says something like, 'I am from Scotland'. But it is not a question of ethnic background. If you ask a black man, he will tell you he is originally from Africa. But I am not talking about Africa. If you identify yourself by your ethnicity, you will be so confused because we are all a mixture of many heritages.

Why am I here? Why do I exist? Why am I on earth? Is there a reason for my life? This is a question of purpose, of destiny.

What can I do? Do you know that 99% of the population of this planet will die without fully realizing their true ability? Science has proved that we only use 10% of our brain power. Imagine—we have built our cities on 10% of our brain power. It is a question of potential.

Where am I going? It is a question of destiny. Where is my future address in life?

These five questions control the entire human race. That is why a man will do two jobs, abandoning his children and frustrating his wife. He tries to find his identity by competing with other people to buy nice cars and nice clothes so that he feels accepted. Why will a young woman sell her body to get money and buy clothes, so she can feel important? Because she is struggling with *'Who am I? Why am I here? Where am I going? What can I do?'"* People do stupid things to try to answer these questions.

We are all created to live life with meaning. No one came to this planet as an experiment. Ignorance of purpose does not cancel out the purpose. Because you do not know why you exist does not mean you do not have a reason for existence. Until you discover your personal reason for being born, your life will be unfulfilled. You will live as an experiment. You will keep trying. The greatest tragedy in life is not death, but it is a life without purpose.

Let us understand what the purpose is!

It is tragic to be alive and not know why you are on earth. The book of Ecclesiastes, written by King Solomon, is a book that makes man discover that what he does is foolish. King Solomon said that a man without purpose is a 'still born' baby.

I quote: "a 'still born' baby is better off than a man without purpose." Because a 'still born' baby does not know where he comes from, never arrives and never goes back. Solomon said it is more tragic for a man to be born from the womb, live on earth, spend years on the planet and then die...and never know why he came. I like the way Solomon opens the book. He says: "everything is meaningless." He says that life is empty. The King James Version uses the word 'vanity'. Vanity means empty of purpose. "When life has no purpose then it is like chasing after winds," says Solomon. It is an exercise of frustration. People get up every morning. They join the same traffic queue. They go to the job they hate. They work more hours. They work for people they do not like. They do things they don't want to do and they go back home full of afflictions. They watch TV programs that depress them, and then they go to bed and sleep back to back with their spouses without speaking to them. They wake up the next morning and they get stuck in the same traffic again. And they do that for 48 years and they retire from a job that they are glad that they have left. And they die; all they did was work to make a living. But they never live. They never exist. That is a tragedy. You are not born to make a living. You are not born just to pay bills. You are not born just to maintain rent. There has got to be more to your life.

Without a purpose, life has no meaning; life has no reason; life has no passion. Helen Keller was born blind and she said that there is something worse than being blind and that is having sight without vision. There are people who have eyes but cannot see. They have no vision in their life.

Nothing is worse in life than the death of a dream. I love what Dr. Myles Munroe says: "The wealthiest place on earth is the cemetery. Why the cemetery? Because buried in the cemetery are books that will never be written. The graveyard is full of music that will never be played. The cemetery is filled with songs that will never be sung. The graveyard is packed with poetry that will never be read. It is filled with businesses that will never be opened. It is filled with ministries that never got started. The cemetery is filled with visions that never become reality. It is the wealthiest place on earth."

The cemetery is packed with treasure. And that treasure is called potential. Potential is defined as untapped power, hidden strength, unused ability. Potential is unused success. It is dormant power. Potential is who you are but no one knows it yet. Potential is what you can do but have not yet done. Potential is how far you can go but have not yet gone.

The minute you have done something, it ceases to be a potential. Potential is never what you have done; it is always what you could do and you have not done it yet. And that is what the graveyard gets. It gets what people have not done yet. And God wants you to die with none of this treasure in you. He wants you to die empty.

Humans are supposed to die old. We are supposed to die finished. Jesus Christ was 32 and one-half years old. He was not an old man. He lived a full life and finished his purpose. He never said on the cross "I am finished." Because we never finish, we are spirit. He said "It is finished." That means you and I came to this planet with an 'it', with an assignment, with a purpose, with a destiny. You came to the planet to deliver that assignment to your generation. You are born to die finished. A cemetery should not get a dream that you are born to deliver to your generation. And life is not measured by its length but it is measured by its accomplishment in God.

Potential is the you that nobody knows yet. Potential is the accomplishment that you are yet to reach. This is why God is never interested in what you have done. God is always interested in what you could do, but have not done yet. That is why the greatest enemy of your success is your last success. Nothing can stop you from progressing more than being impressed with your last success. Some people are so proud of what they have done that they stop doing what they could do. What you have done is not more exciting to God. That is why you should never be so impressed by your past accomplishments that you stop releasing what is left inside you. That is why you have to be cautious when people start giving you rewards and trophies because they can actually be giving you the wrong sense of success. A trophy is a person's measurement of their impression of what you have done. But God is never impressed by what you have done. He is always going after what is left on the inside; because He knows what He put inside of you. That is why he is called 'The God of Faith'. Faith is a substance for things, not that you have done, but what you hope to do and it is an evidence of things, not what people can see, but that are yet not seen. And without faith it is impossible to please your manufacturer, God. We need to be never trapped by our past successes. Your future delivers your true potential and purpose.

The principle of potential is the essence of God himself. God is not God of potential. He is himself potential. There are two words that bear remembering: The first word is OMNI = ALL, or EVERYTHING. The second word is POTENT = POWER, ABILITY, STRENGTH, MIGHT. When you add those 2 words together, it is OMNIPOTENT = ALL POTENTIAL. This word is only applied to God. God is omnipotent. He is always full of unseen abilities. Everything that is...was in God.

Genesis 1:0 says before anything was, God is. If God created everything, then everything came out of God. And if you were to meet God before anything was made, you would be meeting everything because everything is inside of God. That is why God needs to speak everything out of him. He was pregnant with everything. If you cannot see what is in a person that does not mean it is not there. By doing so, you are actually ignoring God.

The principle of releasing everything out of him is called work. It is found in Genesis 2:1–2:

> *1 "Thus the heavens and the earth, and all the host of them, were finished. 2 And on the seventh day God ended His work which He had done, and He rested on the seventh day from all His work which He had done."*

Potential is the result of work performed. If you want to fulfill your purpose, you have to be willing to work. The principle of potential and purpose is introduced by God himself in Genesis 1. It is a first principle of creation. It is found in Genesis 1:11:

> *26 "Then God said, 'Let the land produce vegetation: seed bearing plants and trees on the land that bear fruit with seed in it, according to their various kinds.' And it was so."*

Everything that God created, He created with everything in it that was supposed to be within it. That is why it is called 'seed of principle of potential'. God hides in everything its future. Your future therefore is not ahead of you. It is trapped within you. If you have a mango seed in your hand, and I ask you what it is, you will reply that is a mango seed. The problem is that that is a fact but is not the truth. A fact is defined as a description of the present state of a thing. The truth is defined as the true reality of a thing. So in my hand I have a mango seed because that is what you see and it is only a fact. The truth is I have a mango tree in my hand; because the tree is trapped in the seed. That is called potential. But this is not the complete truth either. In the seed—is the tree and in the tree—is the seed of a mango. That is the mystery of God's potential principle. God never gives you a tree; He always gives you a seed. Let us emphasize this principle with this example: when God gives you a girl or a boy that is not only a boy or a girl but a forest of untapped abilities. That is why God hates abortion. Abortion is not the destruction of a baby but a destruction of a complete destiny.

When you kill a seed, you do not kill a seed, you are destroying a forest. That is why in everything God created He put a seed. God likes to hide things in what he has created. That is called potential. That is why we should never ignore anyone—because we do not know what they are filled with. You should never ignore people, because they are full of purpose and potential. And whatever you are going through right now is not your end. That is why you should not let your life fade away. Do you believe that trapped inside of Paul (a serial killer) was the New Testament?

It does not matter what people are going through; God will never abandon His people. In fact, that is why Jesus died. He died because he knew that salvation is trapped in every human being. Jesus did not only die for you, He died for what you are carrying. He does not only save a person, He saves a complete destiny.

That is why Moses' mum took a risk of saving her baby. She was not only saving a baby, but she was saving the first five books (Torah) of the Bible, she was not just saving the deliverer of millions of people, she was saving one of the greatest leaders of history.

Your destiny must be preserved. If you are divorced, listen! A divorce is just an event but is not your life. If you fail in school, listen! Failure is temporary; your destiny still is in you. You will finish this life college that God has allowed you to study. Get back on the road—study even more. Come back to the Lord. Because your future is within you.

Purpose and potential need pressure to be revealed. You will never know what you can do until you are tested. The future of your destiny is trapped within you. You have to learn how to reach out there and achieve it; don't settle until you have sought everything your heart desires. Do not fear the failure of not achieving...achieve at least the task of trying. Believe that God will provide you all He intends and gain strength and courage from this knowledge. Seek more and you will achieve more. Believe more in God's purpose for you and take less credit of what comes your way. It is He—who provides your breath, your life and your future.

Proverbs 19:21:

> *'Many are the plans in a man's heart, but it is the LORD's purpose that prevails.'*

This verse teaches us 3 things:

1. Purpose is more important than plans.

2. Purpose is more powerful than plans.

3. Purpose precedes plans: God, in others words established the purpose for your lifelong before you were born to make any plans for your life.

Your purpose therefore is the most important thing to God. In fact, God is really not interested in your plans; He is only concerned about His purpose of your life. But there is good news! God's purpose for your life is not to harm you, not to hate you but to give you an expected end. God has a great plan for you and it is this purpose therefore that is the most important thing in life.

The question now is, "What is this purpose?"

Purpose is defined as:

1. Original intention for its existence.

2. Reason for the existence of a thing.

3. The desired result in the mind of the manufacturer.

4. Motivation causing creation of a product.

5. Source of the destination established by manufacturer.

Purpose simply means: WHY. Every time that man asks the question 'why?' he is asking what is the purpose of the thing. Every manufacturer creates a product for a reason. You will never find a manufacturer who creates something and says, "I wonder what I will use it for?" It never happens. A manufacturer begins with a purpose then moves back to the product. He discovers why something must exist and then he creates the thing.

The purpose precedes the production and therefore when the Bible says in the book of Proverbs 19:21: *"Many are the plans in a man's heart, but it is the Lord's purpose that prevails."*

It means that before you were conceived in your mother's womb and before you are born and then later before you make plans, God has already an original intention for you. He has a reason for your existence and he established it before you were born. Therefore, your life is not an experiment; it is not a mistake. You are not a biological accident between your mother and your father. The purpose is more important than anything in your life because it gives you the meaning for your breathing every day.

1. The purpose is the end that started the beginning.

2. The purpose is the finish before the start.

3. The purpose is the destination before the journey.

4. The purpose is the final address for your life: where you are intended to end up.

5. The purpose is the reason for your birth, and your existence.

Without God's purpose for you, life has no reason and your existence has no reason. And that's why most people abuse their life.

Some principles that help to discover your life:

1. ***God is a God of purpose***: God does not do anything without a reason. There is a motivation in everything that God has created.

2. ***The purpose is found in everything***: everything that exists was born for a reason. It was born to perform an assignment. It was born to fulfill a result. Everything performs a function in its creation. Because you do not know the purpose of the thing, it does not mean that it does not have one. The ignorance of the purpose does not cancel the purpose. The scientists have discovered that everything in life serves a purpose. They call it 'Ecologic'. Ecologic is simply man admitting that God has a reason to create, for example, a tree. There is a purpose and a function for everything. If you stop a purpose for one thing, you destroy something else. That is why ecologists tell us not to destroy the rivers, not to pollute the air, not to destroy the Amazon forest...If there is a purpose for a rock and God has the purpose for the mosquito, are you not as valuable as all those things. That is why every human being was born for a purpose.

3. **Not every purpose is known**: because you do not know why you were born does not mean that there is no reason for your birth.

4. **Where purpose is not known, abuse is inevitable**: that means if you do not know the destiny of the thing, you will abuse it. That is why we abuse children. We carry out abortions. Because we do not understand that the baby was conceived for a purpose. When you destroy a child, you are terminating a purpose. You are kill-

ing the future. You are destroying an assignment. Let us take an example: God made marijuana, cocaine, tobacco plants, and He said that they are very good. But then you might ask, "How can things that are very good destroy our community?" Because of two words: **Ab** (normal) and **Use.** These two words together make Abuse. To abuse something means you are using it abnormally. If you use a drug in the hospital, it is called medicine. If you use it on the street, it is called dope. If you use it in the hospital, it gives you health. If you use it in the street, it destroys you. When you abuse the purpose, it is self-destruction. That is why it is important for you to find God's assignment and purpose in your life. Stop abusing your body with alcohol, cigarettes...

Stop abusing your body with things, which you have learned are harmful for you. When you are certain something is not good for you—know that God intends for you not to place it in your body, mind, life.

'FACTS WILL ALWAYS TELL YOU
WHAT YOUR LIMITATIONS ARE,
WHILE FAITH WILL ALWAYS POINT
YOU TO GOD'S LIMITLESSNESS.'

CHAPTER 3

CELEBRATE YOUR UNIQUENESS

The Bible says that without a vision, the people perish (Proverbs 29:18). In other words: without light, without revelation, the people perish. Every one of us came to this world for a reason. You are not an accident in the world. Also, please know that you are not an experiment. God is not trying to find out what you should be or what you will do. He is not trying to find out what you will become. You are not a chance product of your parents.

The Bible says that children are the heritage of the Lord (Psalm 127:3). This scripture means that God gives you to your parents and not that your parents produced you and God found you. Many people believe that we arrived and then God found us. God gave you as a gift of trust to your parents when you were born. Every one of us has to be born. We all came through a man and a woman. In other words, God planned from the foundation of the world that you should come into being and He chose to give you to your parents as a gift of trust.

Ephesians 1:3-6 shows us clearly God's purpose for mankind:

"3 Blessed be the God and Father of our Lord Jesus Christ, who has blessed us with every spiritual blessing in the heavenly places in Christ, 4 just as He chose us in Him before the foundation of the world, that we should be holy and without blame before Him in love, 5 having predestined us to adoption as sons by Jesus Christ to Himself, according to the good pleasure of His will, 6 to the praise of the glory of His grace, by which He made us accepted in the Beloved."

As a child, your parents are responsible for you and to some measure, for what happens to you. Then after you have grown up and fully matured, you will be held responsible for your actions. You are responsible for your life. Parents should show their love but they must have the understanding that there's a limit to their plan for the children. For example, the Bible says in the Book of Proverbs (Ch 22 v6): "*Train up a child in the way he should go.*" The Bible does not say train up a child in the way you want him to go, not in the way society wants him to go but in the way he should go. And the Bible continues: "…And when he is old, he will not depart from it."

How will you train up a child in the way he should go? What way should he go? That means that parents have the responsibility to find out from God the way their child should go and train up the child for the purpose for which he was born. Only God has the knowledge of the purpose for which the child was born.

I believe that everyone has to know the purpose for which he came into this world. God will show you, guide you to the knowledge of the purpose trapped within you.

The statements above help us to understand the reason why a great many of people are frustrated and depressed…because they do not know their reason for being. Depression often comes about because a person has come to the point of just thinking that they simply just exist in the world. The trouble is there are people who never find out in the whole of their lifetime; they never get to know the reason for their coming into this world and they even die without knowing it.

Can you image how many great works of art, music and literature are buried in the graveyard near your house? Can you image how many solutions to the problems we face today are buried with someone you knew? People die without releasing their full potential. They fail to use all that is stored in them for the benefit of the world. The world misses out because they fail to live out their potential. The cemetery is the richest place on earth. There is more to your life.

There can be no life emptier or more frustrating than one that ends without a purpose. It would be a shame to have lived without using or finding the potential in you. When a person finds the reason why he is born, his life has a meaning. He is given a purpose for living.

Find out: Why did you come? Why were you born? Why did you come at this time? Why were you not born 100 years ago? Why not later, in years to come? Why are you here now? One reason is that God wants you to be born at this time is relevant to your generation.

When you do not know the reason for your existence, you live to please somebody else. I remember a story about a young medical doctor. His parents raised him to be a doctor because the father always wanted to be a medical doctor, but it did not work out for him. As the father had always wanted to be a medical doctor, he decided that his son was going to be a really successful senior doctor. Their son was sent to the best school. His parents made a lot of sacrifices to get enough money to raise him well and send him to the best of schools. And finally, he came out as a medical doctor. Oh! How satisfied his parents were. The man was happy to see his dream for life fulfilled in his son. The son began to work as a doctor and he did his job very well. The community in which he lived loved him.

One day, the community decided to give him a reward for being an exceptional medical doctor. They gathered together for a special celebration in the community hall. The parents were so excited, so happy. This was their day to see their son honored with the award: Best doctor in the town. The ceremony started with speech after speech before all the guests. The award was presented to this young doctor. His parents began to feel like the happiest parents in the world. Finally, it was time for the young man to speak. He was given the microphone. He looked straight at the people then turned to his parents and his voice broke. He began to weep. He said: "I do not want it. I am tired. I am fed up." Everybody wondered what could possibly cause him to say such a thing. Some even wondered if something was the matter with him. What was supposed to be a day of joy had suddenly changed.

The young man looked his parents in the eyes and said: "I have lived my entire life trying to fulfill your dream. I never wanted to be a medical doctor. I struggled all my life. You made me a doctor but I have never been happy. I am just living out your dream. Yes, I am thankful for what you have done for me, and yes, even grateful for the sacrifices you have made, but I am not myself. I do not think I deserve this award because I do not know the man who wins it. I do not know myself." He wept. The ceremony chairman helped him leave the platform. Later the young man told his parents that he had always wanted to be a musician but they had made him a doctor.

Here is the point in this story. The young man was living a dream...a desire...for someone else. You can be helped and guided but it is important that the one who helps you knows God's purpose for your life. If he does not know it, he may not have a true intent and he may end up not being able to help you; and this will mess up your life.

It is important to know that you are not a mistake. Your life is not an experiment with God. It is important to know you are so valuable that God would not let you be conceived in your mother's womb unless you were already finished in His mind. God fixed the reason of your existence on earth. You are not a child of choice by your parents. The Bible says God chose you, "in Him." When? *"Before the creation of the World."* (Ephesians 1:4–5). You existed before you manifested. God timed your entrance. He timed your arrival on earth. He also chose you in Him, according to the vision of Him that works everything out through the plan of His purpose. He chose you according to the plan He had for your life. You are not one in a million. He chose you before He made the earth. You are born for a purpose, and the purpose was already finished. Whatever you were born to do is needed in this generation. Whatever you were born to do is supposed to happen in this generation, during this time that you are on earth. You are destined at this particular time to change the atmosphere of your city, your community, your home, your nation, your church. Purpose is timed. Your birth, which is also part of purpose, was timed. Some of you think that you are a mistake, but you are an appointment. If you do not have the character to do what you were born to do, you could be guilty of generational robbery by allowing your gift to remain latent and dormant.

I ask myself every day what is wrong with Africa. The answer does not purely and only revolve around the government. The wrong purpose is the problem of Africa. Africa is living another continent's dream. Africa is not living its own dream but the European-American dream. Africa never determined the purpose of its beautiful nation and African nations are orchestrated to administrate, not to produce.

All journey through life with the idea of getting rich through politics or administration. All want to be administrators, directors, politicians...and they think that prosperity can only be attained if they are in the government. Various people want to get into power. Get the power so you can get the money. We have been wrongly taught that success is in the administration. Not one of us is producing. We must change our mind and our mentality for Africa in order to live its dream.

There is a place for everybody, no matter what you are called to do. In the book of Joel (Chap 2 v 28–29) the Bible records this statement from God:

> 28 *"And it shall come to pass afterward That I will pour out My Spirit on all flesh; Your sons and your daughters shall prophesy, Your old men shall dream dreams, Your young men shall see visions.* 29 *And also on My menservants and on My maidservants I will pour out My Spirit in those days."*

God is telling you that your age will not close your eyes. It will not stop you dreaming. You always have a dream: a dream of success, a dream of victory. God is telling you how you can keep your dreams and that your age is not a limitation. But society makes people lose their dreams because they think that their dreams went with their youth.

Inside every one of us is the desire to be relevant, important and significant. When this desire is wrongly pursued, we get all this anti-social behavior: dictators, robberies, murders, corruptions...You want to be something because you think you are here for nothing. Some have put their family at risk because of this dream to become something, somebody. Everyone is searching. They look for it in their job and in their marriage... they look to get it from somewhere.

Why not stop and ask God the reason for your coming on earth? Why are you not looking to find out if you are on the right road or you are journeying in someone's tracks? Lots of us are living in the shadow of someone else; carrying the burden of pleasing somebody. It does not matter how society acknowledges you but it is what God says about you that really counts. The success of a product is the fulfillment of the purpose for which it was made.

But everyone is created with value. This is why Jesus came and paid such a price for you. Your price is in the blood of God's Son. You are valuable. You know your value by the price Jesus paid. I challenge each and every one of you to find out who you are. Find out the reason for your coming. You are a created being and it is not you who have a purpose for your life. Your creator God is the only one who has it and He is the only one who defines it. The one who created you is the one who has the purpose for your life. Do not live for nothing.

You cannot be jealous of others when you know why you are born. I like the meaning of the signboard. It shows you where to go. It does not go anywhere. It just shows the direction. If you are a signboard from God, you will lead people to where they must go and you will not be jealous. You have only fulfilled your purpose. When you find your purpose, you will not ask for a reward because no one can ever reward you enough. Look at a teacher. He raises men to become doctors, politicians, engineers and he himself never becomes a doctor or an engineer. But he is happy to be in that class. He is excited to see that his pupil from many years ago has become a head of state. A real teacher is excited to see his pupils become a governor, or a lawyer...That is one who is called to be a teacher. He has found his purpose. His joy is to see success and life in all pupils that he has raised. But the one who has a job as a teacher, he is different from the one who has a vocation as a teacher. The teacher with a vision is happy but the one with a job is frustrated. The teacher with a vision will always have pupils who remember him and he will never lack anything. But no one remembers the teacher who only did his job; and he was paid for it and he got mad if he was not paid enough; or wasn't given raises when he felt they were deserved.

Do not let the government, the economics, the system of this world ruins your life. Get the dream, get the vision, get the purpose from God and stay grounded. Become what God made you to be.

The Apostle Paul tells us how the Holy Ghost, who lives in us, is there to show us the way. The Holy Ghost, the Governor, is

bestowed in you to help you to find your origin, your purpose.
1 Corinthians 2:12 (NKJ):

> *12 "Now we have received, not the spirit of the world, but the Spirit who is from God, that we might know the things that have been freely given to us by God."*

I like what one of my spiritual fathers says all the time: "I know who I am." This motto has become part of my daily speech too. I know who I am. I am from God and I only landed in the Congo. Because I know my origin and the purpose of God in me, I cannot be frustrated. I do not have problems but challenges or opportunities to move to the next step of success and experiences. The problems are opportunities to progress for me. I know why I am born.

When you do not know the reason for your being, you become envious, jealous. You fight others. But when you know who you are, you realize that you are unique. No one can take your place nor can you take the place of someone else. You realize that there are no two fingers prints alike in the entire world. No one is like you today and nobody will ever be like you. You are unique. Nobody can do things exactly like you. Nobody can get your kind of results. Get excited about your uniqueness. You are made for this time. This is your hour. This is your time. Rise up and take a challenge...take two, take three; continue believing in you being successful. Rise up and shine. Your light has come and the glory of the Lord is upon you.

The Apostle Paul in his second letter to Timothy (Chap 2 v 20: *"But in a great house there are not only vessels of gold and silver, but also of wood and clay, some for honor and some for dishon-*

or." Paul is telling us how there are different kinds of vessels. What vessel are you? It does not matter whether you are a gold or wood vessel. It is not the kind of vessel that is the problem because he says in verse 2, "if only a man purge himself he will become a vessel unto honor, ready for the master's use." What do you bear? I am a vessel. You are a vessel. You and I are carrying something for this generation. Take a stand. Refuse to be an empty vessel. A vessel carries something. What are you carrying for your generation? Have you looked in that vessel? Have you found out what God put in you? You are carrying something and somebody needs it in this generation and that is why you came to this world.

Things change when you know the purpose for your life. You are on the journey and you know where you are from and where you are going. There is nobody that is strong enough to stop you. No one is powerful enough to hinder you. God has given you a gift that this generation needs. Your success was proclaimed before your coming.

Ephesians 2:10 (Amplified Bible)

> *"For we are God's [own] handiwork (His work-manship), recreated in Christ Jesus, [born anew] that we may do those good works which God predestined (planned beforehand) for us [taking paths which He prepared ahead of time], that we should walk in them [living the good life which He prearranged and made ready for us to live]."*

Do not get carried away with the worldly symbols of success. They are only frustrations. They are roads of sadness and depression. Man does not become his belongings. Jesus said that man's life consists not of the abundance of things he possesses. Man's success is only emptiness. Do not look for success but look to be a man of value. No one was created to be a failure. Have you seen any manufacturer that designs his product for failure and sends you a warranty for the failure of his product? So why would God do that? Why will God produce you with the symbols of failure? Why will He produce you and create something that will destroy you? God is committed to your success. He is more keen on your success than you ever could have been.

This is a time of decision, of reflection: Who am I? Why did I come? Where am I going? It is a time to answer. It is a time to discover all that God wants of me. A true success is when you become what God made you to be. This is the time of change. Change your belief system. Change your mind. Refuse to be unusual because some people have written themselves as unusual. Never let somebody limit you because of your skin, because of the country where you were born, because of your family. You are a child of God and please have a consciousness of what you are.

I love what my mentor Dr. Myles Munroe wrote in his book, "Daily Power and Prayer." He is showing us how God is our power supply and we should be attached to this power. Dr Myles writes that in 2004, a monster storm attacked the beautiful Island of the Bahamas and the electricity went off. As he examined the rooms where he had television, VCR, CD players, air conditioners, computers...he noticed that there was no flash of light and all those items were completely useless because of the power failure. And he thought about the power, potential, benefits, pleasure and untapped functions trapped in each of these items that were completely useless at that moment. The items were filled to capacity with possibility, but they could not deliver. Why? Because they were cut off from their source, their power supplies. He then saw a true picture of mankind. A powerful creature full of divine potential, talents, gifts, abilities, untapped capacity, creativity, ingenuity, and productivity. But unless man is connected to God, his true abilities lie dormant inside him. Man can fulfill his true potential and maximize his full capacity only by remaining connected to his creator.

Not only are all things composed of that from which they came, they must also remain attached to that source in order to live. The minute a plant decides it does not like the earth anymore, it dies. The minute the fish decide they are tired of water, they die. The minute animals decide, "We don't want to eat from the dirt anymore," they begin to die. Thus, whatever God created came from that to which He spoke. All things were created by God's word to source. The source of the creation also becomes, then, the essence of that creation. All things are composed of whatever they came from and hence contain the potential of that source. When God wanted fish, He spoke to the water. When He wanted animals, He spoke to the dirt. When God created human beings, He spoke to Himself.

> 26 *"Then God said, "Let Us make man in Our image, according to Our likeness; let them have dominion over the fish of the sea, over the birds of the air, and over the cattle, over all the earth and over every creeping thing that creeps on the earth." 27 So God created man in His own image; in the image of God He created him; male and female He created them." Genesis 1:2627 (NKJ).*

God created you by speaking to Himself. You came out of God and thus bear His image and likeness. Never use the creation to find out who you are, because the purpose of something is only in the mind of the One who made it. You will never know yourself by relating to the creation, only to the Creator. The key to understanding life is in the source of life, not in the life itself. If you want to know who you are, look at God. You are who you are because God took you out of Himself. Stay connected to your power supply. Prayer and communion with God give us the power we need to fulfill our purposes in Him.

'ALL OF OUR LIVES WE HAVE BEEN
TOLD WHAT WE COULD NOT DO, AND
TOO OFTEN WE TAKE THAT AS FACT.'

CHAPTER 4

DO NOT BE LIMITED BY THE SYSTEM

The system here is defined as the normal way things are done: You go to work, get a pay check and then pay your bills…

The world has set the path that you must follow. But you have dreams and desires which you cannot see becoming a reality because you think that you don't have the right connections, the right education. These limitations that you have most likely placed on yourself make you think that you will never rise any higher. You most likely are limited by your own system that you are part of at this time.

One thing you should know is that our God likes to go 'outside the system'. He likes you to do unusual, extraordinary things. No matter where you are in life, no matter what environment you are in, no matter how impossible your dream may seem, you need to know that God already has a plan and a way for you. If you stay in Faith, God will go 'outside the system' and take you to a place that you never knew existed.

When God needed a king for Israel, He did not choose the most qualified person. He did not go to the most influential family or choose an experienced military leader, someone with great knowledge and expertise. Instead, He found a teenager, a young shepherd boy who was out taking care of his father's sheep. And He chose that young man, David, to be the next king. God likes to take ordinary people and use them to do extraordinary things.

I would like to encourage you to not limit yourself. Don't be limited by the 'system'. You may look around today and think your dream will never come true. Perhaps you don't have the money; you don't have the education; you come from a poor family, a poor area…No! Actually, you are just the kind of person that God loves to use. Instead of being discouraged by all of these things you should turn them around and be encouraged knowing you are prime material for God to use.

At the time when Jesus chose his twelve disciples, Sadducees and Pharisees were the most prestigious religious leaders. They studied religion, law and tradition and were very influential. They walked around the city in distinguished robes and they got the best seats at ceremonies. But it's interesting that Jesus did not choose any of them as his disciples. He chose neither the most qualified nor the most educated, nor even the most influential. Certainly, God can make great use of people like that—it's good to have education and influence—but very often, He will do things outside the traditional, ordinary way. A prime example was when Jesus ended up choosing a fisherman and a tax collector. He chose the equivalent of business people, carpenters and school teachers. He went 'outside the system' to choose his disciples to do extraordinary things.

Do not allow where you are in life right now and the things that are not going your way to cause you to give up on your dreams. It may not happen overnight, but if you stay in Faith, God will move heaven and earth to get you to where you are supposed to be. No person can keep you from your destiny, except you. No obstacle can keep you from accomplishing your dream. It may look impossible to you, but God can do the impossible. Stay in Faith and remain firm in your belief. When God puts the promise in your heart, it does not matter how it appears to everyone else; it does not matter who criticizes your system; it does not matter what obstacles get in your way—stay faithful and you will see that God will make it come to pass.

Look at Mary, the mother of Jesus—a teenage girl living in a town called Nazareth. It was the poorest city in that region. You would think that if God were going to choose somebody to give birth to His son, He would surely choose someone from a better location, from a more prestigious environment. But wrong again! God went 'outside the system'. He did not choose a prominent, influential young lady. Mary was just a common girl living in an average family in a lower income neighborhood.

Luke 1:30–31:

> *30 "Then the angel said to her, "Do not be afraid, Mary, for you have found favor with God. 31 And behold, you will conceive in your womb and bring forth a Son, and shall call His name JESUS."*

Mary said this was impossible. She couldn't have a baby without a man. It was outside the law of nature.

The answer of the angel (Luke 1:35 "*And the angel answered and said to her, "The Holy Spirit will come upon you, and the power of the Highest will overshadow you; therefore, also, that Holy One who is to be born will be called the Son of God."*") shows how God goes 'outside the system' to do something:

I love what Mary said. (Luke 1:38: "*Then Mary said, "Behold the maidservant of the Lord! Let it be to me according to your word." And the angel departed from her."*)

In that moment the seed took its place in her heart.

When God gives us a promise it may not make any sense to our mind. It may be out of the ordinary, but if we can do just as Mary did…say, "God, I receive it. It may currently look impossible; but God, I know that you can do the impossible…not only for others, but you can also do them for me. So I come in agreement with you and I believe that it will happen just as you say."

It is interesting that Mary asked how it could happen without a man. Her question was a natural one. But there is a deeper meaning. God is saying that you don't have to have people to see your dream come to pass. Your friend may not believe in your dream; your colleagues may think that you don't have what it takes; your own family may think that you just are wasting your time; but the good news is that God does not need them to bring that promise to fulfillment. Do not allow people to take you out of what you feel on the inside. Your dream is not dependent on other people. God is saying it can happen without a man, without a banker, without a doctor, without a boss and certainly without the approval of your family, friends, etc. It can happen in spite of what people say. YOU AND GOD ARE THE MAJORITY.

Psalm 75:6:

'For not from the east nor from the west nor from
the south come promotion and lifting up'. (KJV)

This means that promotion does not come from people. It does not come from your boss or the people around you but it comes from almighty God. When God is ready to promote you, ready to take you to the new level, it does not matter what you do or do not know, it will happen. No person can stand against our God. You may not know the right people but you do know the right God and that is all that really matters. Your dream is not dependent on other people.

When you get 'outside the system', do not be surprised if you face judgment and criticism. Do not be surprised when people start talking ill of you. When you have a big dream in your life, it disturbs small-minded people. They get jealous. They are intimidated. They are so insecure that they feel they have to push you down so they can feel important. They do not realize God has an individual plan for each of us. We are not all going to give birth to the son of God. He chose Mary for that. But I have to be big enough to celebrate what is going on in other people's lives at the same time as knowing that God has a great plan in store for me. He has not left any of us out.

That is what happened to Mary. Everybody started talking about her pregnancy. You can image what she went through; all that gossip — people talking behind her back about her having a baby without being married. Even her fiancé Joseph wanted to walk away when he heard that Mary was pregnant. Mary had to endure all that criticism and all that ridicule but she did not allow them to trouble her. She kept her eyes on the prize.

So many people try to defend themselves and convince everyone that they are right. You need to know that no matter how sincere you are, there will be people who are never going to agree with you.

Not everyone has to accept you and not everyone is going to understand you. Do not spend all your time trying to win over your critics but just continue in your ways. Because God did not put the promise in them that He put in you, you cannot expect them to understand. Look at Jesus; He was one of the most controversial and criticized person that ever lived. He got more criticism from the religious crowd than from the secular crowd. The Sadducees and the Pharisees were so small-minded and they were only polishing their doctrines; thinking that they knew everything. They spent their time trying to push Jesus out when He was at work changing the world, bringing hope, healing, making a difference. They were constantly trying to find fault in Jesus. There are Sadducees and Pharisees still alive today. They are the people who always find fault when you do something out of their norm. These are the people that will tell you that what you are doing is wrong.

We need to learn to act like Jesus. Just shake it off and move on. You may always be controversial but just remember if God says that it has to happen, there is nothing other people can do to keep it from happening. I have learned that the pain and discomfort you feel when things are against you actually mean you are near your goal.

The enemy will not fight you so hard if he does not already know that God is about to do something which He has never done before in your life. The enemy does not oppose you because of where you are but because of where you are going. He does not fight you for the present; he fights you for the future. Maybe it is in your health life that the enemy attacks you; the promise that God is restoring your health is coming to you right now in Jesus' name. You are coming out of this sickness. Your mind will tell you that you are wrong. Nobody has ever done this before but you can be the first. With God all things are possible. The doctor may have told you that there is nothing that science can do but I have good news for you: men have nothing to do with the promise of what is coming to pass. It is not up to people. It is up to God.

The bible says that there was no room for Mary to give birth. In today's language we would say there were no hospitals available, no clinic, no hotel, and not even a home. But Mary was so full of that promise she knew that great things could happen 'outside the system'. She basically went where the animals lived and gave birth to the son of the living God. When the time comes for your promise to be born, all the forces of darkness will not be able to stop it happening. The system may not let you in but God will go 'outside the system' to make it happen. Sometimes the system is too small for your dream. Sometimes God has to move you away from the people around you because they are limiting you. Maybe you will not like it but God knows that He has to get you out of that limited environment. You may feel today that the system is pushing you out. Door after door keeps closing. But I want to let you know that sometimes God closes doors because you think too small and He feels that where you are in your life right now is there because you have been thinking and believing in small things for yourself. Enlarge your vision and you will see the enormity of what God wants to do in you. You may have dreams in your heart and they are bigger than your finances, bigger than your education, bigger than what your family has ever done. Be encouraged today that God specializes in going 'outside the system' to do extraordinary things.

Remember! God loves to take ordinary people and use them to do extraordinary things. You have not yet seen your best day. Remember! Facts will always tell you what your limitations are, while Faith will always point you to God's limitlessness. Facts are often the precursor of fear. The enemy will use facts to steal your peace and take your focus off of God's Faithfulness.

KNOWING YOURSELF

The greatest discovery in human experiences is self-discovery. Your true being comes alive when you become aware of your true nature. The great Greek philosopher Socrates made 'Know thyself' the guiding principle of his life, and this idea was perpetuated by his disciple, Plato. Yet 'know thyself' is an incomplete idea because all they knew was that there was something to learning about yourself. They did not fully understand or explain how to do this. The only way to know yourself is to know where you originated because you are just like the source from which you came. Here is the 'principle of source and resource' by which all creations are subject: *A thing consists of the same material from which it came and must remain attached to its source in order to live and maximize its potential.* This is why the best way to discover and understand yourself is to discover and study the nature and attributes of God.

Needing to know God does not have to do with 'religion' or some of the things people do in the name of religion. It has to do with being introduced to your true self. Only your source can give you an understanding of who you are since you have the same nature and essence that he does. Knowing God leads to humanity greatest knowledge about itself. When a person gets to know his Creator, and finally comes to know himself, then his true Being is born. When he makes this discovery, his attitudes are adjusted. His beliefs about himself, mankind, and his role in the world are radically transformed.

Much of what you have previously heard and accepted as truth has negatively influenced your image of yourself, your beliefs about your worth, and how you have lived your life. We are what we think. Also, we become what we continue to think. You cannot rise above the plane of your mental conditioning. To change your life, you must change your mind. You are a product of your thoughts. There is nothing as powerful as a thought or idea, but there is nothing more important than the source of our thoughts. Our thoughts are products of what we have heard or learned. What we derive our thoughts from determines the kind of thoughts we conceive and who we eventually become. The Bible says that as a person thinks in his heart, so is he. That means the source from which man gets the thoughts that he thinks is most critical. The heart here is not what most people immediately think of the physical organ that beats in our chests. The Hebrew word translated heart is 'Leb', which means 'the feelings, the will, and even the intellect' or the 'inner man'. The heart is usually referring to our subconscious minds and their contents. The heart or subconscious mind is like a computer hard drive. It is the drive on which you have downloaded the software of your experiences and the information that you have received and accepted, as well as your evaluation of them. It stores all your ideas, beliefs, convictions, philosophy, experiences, memories, regrets, hurts and secret thoughts. Whatever you put on your hard drive is what comes out when you press the right buttons. In other words, you take out what you put in. That's why it is important for you to get the right information.

You are what you believe. Your thoughts create your beliefs. A new belief system for you would be — know and understand 100% that your beliefs create your convictions, your convictions create your attitude, your attitude controls your perception and your perception dictates your behavior. What you truly believe about yourself creates your world. Remember that no one can live beyond the limits of his or her beliefs. In other words, your life is what you think it should be. If the source of your thoughts is not correct, then your thoughts are incorrect and your conclusions and beliefs are defective and contaminated — or soon will be. The result is a life lived in error and insecurity.

All of us are in pursuit of something. The most important pursuit in life is the pursuit of the truth. Jesus said that we shall know the truth and the truth shall make us free (John 8:32). The question I asked myself when I read this scripture is: free from what? Jesus knows that whatever we learned before we received His information must be reviewed with suspicion and, if necessary, deleted from our belief systems.

The adversary of God and man is commonly referred to as the 'prince of darkness'. His power to control or to rule a human spirit is generated by our ignorance. Man without the original knowledge of himself from the manufacturer is like a lamp or a candle without a flame. The book of Proverbs tells us that *'the spirit of a man is the lamp of the Lord, searching all the inner depths of his heart* (Prov.20:27)'. What happens when the light of that candle goes out? It needs to be relit. It needs original knowledge. Until God gives a human being the original knowledge of who he is, then he is a candle without a flame. He exists, but he has no real life. He does not have illumination about the way he has been designed. The source is the authority and sustainer of the product. God is your source.

'YOU ARE NEVER TOO OLD TO
SET ANOTHER GOAL OR TO
DREAM A NEW DREAM.'

CHAPTER 5

ONE OF THE GREATEST TRAGEDIES IN LIFE

One of the greatest tragedies in life is to watch potential die untapped.

God said that His people perish by the lack of knowledge (Hosea 4:6). The word 'knowledge' in Greek means light. The opposite of knowledge is ignorance. 'Ignorance' in Greek means darkness. There is death and chaos in darkness. Ignorance is deadly. Ignorance perpetuates disease, poverty and failure. Ignorance produces constant loss in our lives.

Dr. Myles Munroe quoted this paragraph in one of his books:

"The wealthiest spot on this planet is not the oilfields of Kuwait, Iraq, or Saudi Arabia. Neither is it the gold and diamond mines of Republic democratic of Congo (country name changed by the author), the uranium mines of the Soviet Union, or the silver mines of Africa. Though it may surprise you, the richest deposits on our planet lie just a few blocks from your house. They rest in your local cemetery or graveyard. Buried beneath the soil within the walls of those sacred grounds are dreams that never came to pass, songs that were never sung, books that were never written, and paintings that never filled a canvas. Also there are ideas that were never shared, visions that never became reality, inventions that were never designed, plans that never went beyond the drawing board of someone's mind, and purposes that were never fulfilled. Our graveyards are filled with potential that remained potential. What a tragedy".

The greatest tragedy in life is not death, but a life that never realizes its full potential. You must make the decision today not to rob the world of the rich, valuable, potent, untapped resources locked away within you. Potential never has a retirement plan.

Consider the acorn. Each tiny acorn has the potential to grow into a huge oak tree. God created everything with potential, including you. He placed the seed of each thing within itself (see Genesis 1:12), and planted within each person or thing He created the ability to be much more. Thus, everything in life has potential. Take a look at the invisible state in you, because that is the real you. Everything that man has ever seen first existed in an invisible state. (Please note that invisible does not mean non-existent.) By faith God spat out what was in him. Everything in Him started to spring forth. What we now see was given life by God from what was invisible within Him. Whatever you see came from the unseen. Thus, Faith is not the evidence of things that do not exist. It is the evidence of things that are not yet seen. Your Faith is the gateway to your future. Believe in the picture that you see inside you. It is you. Believe it. Speak it out. And become what you see in yourself.

Do you know that you are not just someone born in a ghetto over the hill or a young lady born on a farm in Iowa? There's a wealth of potential in you. The spirit of God, which is connected to your spirit, is the only true judge of your worth. Don't accept the opinions of others because they do not see what God sees. You need to know that life is governed by laws.

Let me quote some of these laws:

- The law of Promotion teaches—You can only be promoted by someone whose instructions you have followed.

- The law of Reproduction indicates—You can only reproduce something you are.

- The law of The Seed reveals—Whatever you have in your hand will create anything you want in your future.

- The law of Recognition—Everything you need in your life is already in your life merely waiting for your recognition.

God operates by those laws and He is the one who established them. He used the law of Recognition in the different people He chose for His primary purpose—to extend the Kingdom of Heaven on earth. The law of Recognition is simple but explosive and hides the key to success. It teaches you that everything you need is already in you and needs only your recognition of it; that anything unrecognized remains uncelebrated by you; that anything you refuse to celebrate eventually exits your life... a miracle, a person etc.

God looked at Adam and saw a world. He looked at Abraham and saw nations. In Jacob, a deceiver, He saw a Messiah. In Moses, the murderer, God saw a deliverer. Can you imagine looking at a stammering young man and seeing the greatest leader in history? God saw a king in a shepherd boy. When the Israelites wanted a king, God sent the Prophet Samuel to the home of Jesse. All the sons of Jesse came before Samuel, from the greatest to the least. Finally, after Jesse had paraded all of his sons before him, Samuel said, "I am sorry. None of these are God's choice for king. Do you have any other sons?" Then Jesse said, "Yes… well, no. I have just remembered. I do have a little boy, my youngest son. He is just a little runt who is out taking care of the sheep".

"Bring him to me," Samuel replied. "Let me look at him."

So, Jesse sent for his youngest son. When Samuel saw Jesse's youngest son walks into the house, a little boy, he began to unscrew the lid of his flask of anointing oil. "I think I have found the person I am looking for," Samuel said.

Most of us are like Jesse. We look, but we don't see. Maybe your family has told you that you are a 'nobody'. Have you been put off and put out and told so many times that you will amount to nothing that you have begun to believe it? Do you feel like the black sheep? Are you someone who repeatedly says aloud that your life is just full of bad luck? Do you feel you are always at the wrong place at the wrong time? It would be incredible for you to learn that not everyone lives believing they are anything but the best that God has made.

I have good news for you today! You are probably the one person in your house that God is waiting for. God sees things deep within you that others can't see. They look at you and may themselves see a nobody; however, God looks at you and sees a worthwhile somebody. You may spend your whole life competing with others or attempting to be like others only to prove that you are somebody and yet still feel like nobody. Free yourself from limiting feelings today! You do not have to live with that feeling any longer. You don't have to try to be somebody, because you already are somebody. There is something you are not seeing in your life today...and it could be costing you dearly.

Since you are full of potential, you should not be the same person next year that you are this year. People who die without achieving their full potential rob their generation of their latent ability. To die with ability that has not been able to be realized and lived to its fullest is irresponsible.

What will the world lack because you fail to live out your potential? God packaged some things in you for the good of the world—use them. Our Potential is the dormant ability, reserved power, untapped strength and unused success God designed into each of us. What I see when I look at you is not the whole you. It is only what you have become so far. Your Potential is much greater than what you are right now. What you will become is much more than we could ever believe now. You are somebody because you came out of God, and some of Him has flowed into you.

- Some of the greatest gifts of your life have not yet been recognized.

- God has put something close to you that you have not seen.

- Failure to recognize the gift is costing you an incredible amount.

Find what God has planted in you, what your potential is. You are here on an assignment. What you love the most reveals the greatest gifts you contain. What you love to talk about, think about and learn about is your place of assignment.

You will only succeed when your assignment becomes an obsession. That is why Apostle Paul says in Philippians 3:13–14:

> '*13 Brethren, I do not count myself to have apprehended; but one thing I do, forgetting those things which are behind and reaching forward to those things which are ahead, 14 I press toward the goal for the prize of the upward call of God in Christ Jesus.*' (NKJV)

The tragedy in life is not death. Actually, the real tragedy is a life without purpose. Destiny is to be discovered, not to be decided. God has already developed a plan for your life. You must enter His presence to discover it.

> '*I know the thoughts that I think toward you*' *(Jeremiah 29:11)*.

Remember, nobody else is aware of all the gifts the Holy Spirit has placed within you. A school teacher said to a boy called Myles Munroe that he had a monkey brain and he would do nothing in life. The boy became Dr. Myles Munroe, a motivational speaker known all over the world. A young Afro-American was continually told that he would never make it in life. This young man later won an Olympic Gold medal and became a world class boxer. Today, he is a pastor of a very dynamic church. He is Georges Foreman. It is not man who created you but God.

You need to have that pioneering spirit...it is easy to be lost in life. You think that you have reached your limits. The truth is that you may be believing that you cannot go farther in your career, in your business, in your projects... But that is not true. As long as you are breathing, you have potential that you have not yet tapped into. You can rise higher than you are. There is a hidden treasure that is dormant in you. When God created you, He not only breathed His life in you, but He planted a part of Himself in you. He put in you everything you need to fulfill your destiny. You have the seed of greatness just waiting to take root and grow. If you want to tap into this treasure, you need to have a pioneering spirit. You can achieve what no one in your family has ever achieved. You can accomplish things that you have thought impossible. Hear me when I say: you have talents and abilities that have not yet come to the fore. My challenge to you, through this book, is that you should not die with the treasure still buried within you. The gift to yourself and to this world is to release a treasure that has been locked up on the inside.

Do not be surprised if you feel that you are not qualified or able to do this, but when you take the step of faith, God will give you strength. He will give your ability and favor. God has already placed in you exactly what you need. He will never give you the desire if you do not already have what it takes. If you rise up in faith with boldness, with confidence, you begin to see new gifts, new abilities, and new talents. They are in you and you just have to work with God to release them.

If you want to walk on water, you need to get out of the boat. When Peter walked on water, there were other disciples in the boat with the potential to do the same. Why was Peter the only one who ended up being able to do this? It is because

Peter was the one willing to get out of his comfort zone and try something that he had never tried before. He was the only one to release his potential. You have the potential in you right now for every opportunity that God brings your way. But you need to do like Peter and get out of your safe zone and get into the failed zone. That is where you know that you need God's help. God wants to amaze you with His goodness. He wants to take you to the places that you think impossible. Do not be satisfied with where you are right now. Do not get too comfortable where you are right now. God wants to move you to the next level.

This book will help you to release untapped potential by stepping into the unsafe territories. You may have had some great victory in the past, but let me tell you, you have not seen anything yet. God never performs His greatest things in your yesterday; they are still in your future. You are a child of God and you have inside you unlimited opportunities. You need to have that pioneering spirit.

Why is it that you do not believe that you have what it takes? Adopt the attitude of 'I know who I am. I am anointed. I am equipped. I am empowered. I am creative. No obstacle is too high for me if I accept what God has in store for me. No challenge is too difficult.' Do not get complacent. Make a demand on your potential and you will be amazed at what you can accomplish.

You should not compete against your friends but you should compete against yourself. Stir up your gifts from the inside. Get ready! Be a pioneer! Be open-minded and expect good things to come your way.

Maybe something looks too big to you and you ask yourself how you can do it. But let me tell you that the Bible says in the book of Zechariah 4:6:

> '*Not by might nor by power, but by My Spirit, says the LORD of hosts*'.

You with the love and the addition of God's purpose for you are the most powerful. Do not let people destroy what you have inside. You will always have opposition, rejection, discouragement but remember that you are a child of the highest God, filled with the seed of greatness.

I really believe that God does not want our life to stagnate. This is why He continues to give us new opportunities. We should make it our goal that we are not going to die with any treasure left on the inside. God chose Joshua when Moses died. Joshua did not know where to start. He faced all the challenges that we face today. But God said to him: 'be strong and courageous' (Joshua 1:6). God was calling out the courage that He had already deposited in Joshua. He knew Joshua was well able. He knew that he could do it. You can call out the good things that God put in you. Call out strength, call out excellence, call out favors, call out determination...they are already in you but you need to release them. What are you calling out over your future, your life? Instead of giving in to defeat, mediocrity and failure in your life and your future, it will be much more miraculous if you start thinking, 'I am blessed; I have the favor of God...' Set your thoughts going in the right direction.

We believe in our heart that we can aim high but it is our mind and our nature that try to limit us by telling us that it is impossible. I know that the scripture says when two of you agree it creates an atmosphere for things to happen. I know that technically that means getting another person to agree with you, but I believe that if you simply get your mind to agree with your heart and you come to an agreement with yourself, then God can and will do great things. The great things He will do for you are most likely things He has already planned but you are just now going to get out of the way of...thereby allowing your life to accept what God has had in store for you all along.

At times, you will find it very difficult to find anyone to agree with you. You never know unless you try. If you wait for all your circumstances, all your friends and all your family to get behind you, you will never develop your great potential. It is great when people are behind you; but if at this time there is no one, just get in agreement with yourself. Do not fear because God is right with you. It is not over until God says it is over. Do not let your past keep you from progressing further.

Your potential has been put in you by your Manufacturer, your Creator, Almighty God. Whether you use it or not does not diminish your full potential, but it does impact your future. The events of your past do not reduce your potential. Maybe you have been through some disappointments, or have had some unfair things happen in life. None of that affects your real potential—the one that has been put in you permanently by the creator of the Universe. When you believe, you take a step of faith and stretch yourself; that is when you start to tap into it. That is when you will rise higher.

'COURAGE IS THE CAPACITY TO GO FROM FAILURE TO FAILURE WITHOUT LOSING ENTHUSIASM.'

SIR WINSTON CHURCHILL

CHAPTER 6

DEVELOPING THE RIGHT ANCHOR THOUGHTS

In this chapter we will see the importance of getting rid of a negative mindset. Every one of us has what we will call anchor thoughts. These are the anchor thoughts that we believe about ourselves. They have to do with our self-image; how we approach life. These thoughts come with us and we do not normally think about them on purpose. People believe their anchor thoughts for so long that they simply and without a great deal of purpose, follow them. The problem with some people is that their anchor thoughts are negative. Usually the type of negative thoughts that people believe about themselves are: *I am not disciplined, I am not attractive,* or thoughts even more harsh such as, *I will never get out of this problem.*

When locked into a specific negative way of thinking, people do not usually always realize that it is their own thinking that is keeping them in this negative atmosphere. Of course, people cannot have negative anchor thoughts and expect to live a positive life.

The types of positive thoughts to have on a daily basis are: I am blessed; I am victorious; I am valuable; I am talented; people like me. Another healthy thought pattern would include: I have the favor of God; God is bringing to me the exact type of life truly right for me at this time.

One solid fact is that if you are going to live in victory, your anchor thoughts have to be positive. In order to do this my advice would be for you to pay more attention to what comes up in you naturally. What do you expect each day? Do you start each day with enthusiasm and excitement? Or do you just hang around and believe and then say aloud that enthusiasm will not work? How do you feel about yourself? Deep down inside yourself are you pleased with who you are on a daily basis? Do you know deep down in your core that you are valuable? Are you proud of your accomplishments? God wants all of His children to be proud of their accomplishments and He wants them to live their life knowing that it has been molded for them to live their fullest.

If you do not get rid of the wrong thoughts, they will set limits in your life. The good news is that everyone is able to develop new anchor thoughts. The way we do it is to prevent negative thoughts from coming back. Repetitive negative thinking is a real drain on spiritually enthusiastic lives. Instead of dwelling on the idea that nothing can be done, thinking hopelessly and letting that thought take root, step back and take extra time out of your schedule. Practice using special intentions.

To gain a positive way of thinking, turn whatever thoughts you are having at the same time 'round to get on the offensive. Begin declaring the Word of God upon us: *I'm having a great day. My future is great. I am forgiven. God is pleased with me.* Statistics show that when asked, people do not generally say,

"I'm having an awesome 'day' or 'life'. The normal answer is: *I'm doing okay.* Or some will just simply declare, *okay, I guess.*

To begin changing your life and to bring positive energy into your belief system about what God truly does intend for you… speak words of faith over your life. That is the best way to get rid of the negative anchor thoughts and form a new and positive one. Even if you do it without speaking aloud, you can interrupt the negative thoughts by speaking out the opposite. So many people today are stuck on the road of life. They do not realize that it is not normal to feel wrong about themselves. Many individuals have been negative either in their thought patterns or in their actual speech for so long that only the negative and taxing/wrong thoughts occur naturally.

Change is the answer. Though it takes work to change your behavior and the way you think and believe, the first step is in being able to make a commitment and to decide to begin noticing when you have a negative thought or when you are about to state a negative aloud and do and practice the opposite thought. Speak it to someone. Look at the next person who asks, "How are you today?" Answer them with, "I'm doing fantastic. It's truly an awesome day." Watch the reaction you get. This can only lead to positive energy, which in the end will be good for both the speaker and the one spoken to at the time. Chances are too that they will pass this mood on to those they interact with that day.

We have to reprogram ourselves with the right information. Our mind is just like a computer. You can buy an expensive and powerful computer with the greatest memory capacity but if you program that computer with the wrong software, it will not function properly. We hear daily about computer viruses. They can get into a perfectly good computer and start to contaminate the software. They make your computer run slow. You cannot access your files. All those problems occur not because it's not a good computer but because somebody reprograms the software. Somebody messes about with the inside and lets the virus slip inside the hard drive. In the same way, you and I are made in the image of almighty God. He is our manufacturer.

When God created us, He made us to be victorious. We have been programmed for success, for joy and for happiness. But the problem is that we sometimes allow the enemy to get in and reprogram our *software*: our mind. Everyone makes the mistake of believing in his/her lies like: *You will never be successful; you will not make it in life*...All this junk contaminates our software.

As a mind goes through life inputting negatives and belief systems that do not actually create a positive world for them, they begin. We lose self-confidence, self-esteem, which causes us to feel inferior. We need to understand that there is nothing wrong with us. Just like the perfectly good computer that is infected by a virus, you are not a mistake, you are not a failure. When God created you, He made you good. The problem is not the hardware but the software. Changing our way of thinking is what will bring about a new life, one worth living and enjoying. The product is the proof that the manufacturer exists. Go back to the manufacturer to find the essence of the product.

You have to know deep down inside you that you have a value, and no matter what problems you come up against you are a victor and not a victim. I know people who have been through rejection and unfairness and they have allowed that negative disc to play over and over again. They soon became burdened with low self-esteem. Possibly, you have been a victim of injustice and you may have even suffered rejection, but this is still not a good reason to allow anyone or anything to keep you from knowing who you really are. You are a child of the most high God. God has breathed His very life into you. You have his royal blood flowing through your veins.

People may try to oppress you; you may even be in an abusive relationship—but understand that this does not change who you are. Once you know the truth about yourself, you will be stronger and you will make more positive decisions. You still are His most prized possession. It does not matter how unfair life has been to you, God still has a great plan for you. He still has you in the palm of His hand.

In Jeremiah 1: 5 God says:

> *"Before I formed you in the womb I knew you;*
> *Before you were born I sanctified you; I ordained*
> *you a prophet to the nations."*

God knew you and planned out your life before you arrived on the planet Earth. You are not a mistake or an accident. Each of God's children was formed to be a part of the divine destiny. Take on the thought process that you specifically have been given an assignment by our heavenly Father. Know that He brought you here on purpose and part of that reason is because there is something that only you can accomplish. That is why your finger print is unique. You are an original. God has already accepted you and approved you.

I love what David said in Psalm 27:10: '*When my father and my mother forsake me, then the Lord will take care of me*'.

Do not let what happened in your past contaminate your software, your thinking.

I once heard the story of a lady that constantly struggled with her life. On a daily basis, she went around with no sense of purpose. She found out that this insecurity came from the fact that she was born to unmarried parents. Upon careful examination of her birth certificate, the woman noticed that the little box marked 'illegitimate' was ticked. That word contaminated her brain, affected her thinking as a child and as a teenager. Even though the woman got married, she felt so insecure. Every time she tried to move on, the idea would come into her mind that she was a mistake and her life would begin to feel like a burden again. The words 'You are not legitimate' kept recurring and almost as if it were automatic, the woman began to believe it. Her personality was affected. Her marriage was affected. One day, she heard a Pastor preaching that the worth and the value of man do not come from people but came from almighty God. She felt that something had exploded inside her.

Scripture says that you shall know the truth and it shall make you free (John 8:32). On that day she recognized that there was one thought holding her captive. She decided to do something about it. When that lie came back into her mind, instead of dwelling on it and letting it depress her, she started talking back to the enemy. She said: *No! I am not a mistake. I am not an accident. God chose me before the creation of the world. I am valuable. I am accepted. I know that I am worthy of a good future, no matter what my birth certificate says. I know I am legitimate.* She started speaking the words of Faith and began to form a new self-image. Soon, she began to see herself as God sees her. Of course, the change did not happen overnight. Instead, little by little, she grew in confidence. Today, this troubled woman is totally free of the destructive ways her mind and belief system had previously reacted to life's situations. The fact is that she could still be back where she was if she had not made this decision to rise up and shake off the negative and destructive thoughts. If you are currently struggling with these types of things, you can do the same today. It was not the truth that set her free but the knowledge of the truth.

By reading this book, I declare to you that today is a new day. Draw a line under the old day; set a goal and begin to shake off destructive thoughts. Work on one day at a time and one thought at a time until you see and feel an improvement. With the proof of each improvement, you will be glad to start declaring every day: *I am in the palm of God. I have a great future and destiny. I know that good things are stored in me.*

A survey was carried out on children between the ages of 2 years and 4 years. It was found that 95% of them were highly creative and capable of abstract thought and imagination. The researchers were amazed at the high percentage of bright, intelligent and innovative children. What was interesting was that when they tested those same children at 7 years of age, they found only 5% were still highly creative. The conclusion was very simple. The children had been reprogrammed by 'the life race'. They had been told what they could not do and what they could work to become. They became limited in their outlook and developed negative anchor thoughts. The fact is that the same thing can happen to every one of us if we don't stay on the offensive.

Life has a way of trying to pull us down through rejection and disappointment. If we are not careful, we will not be able to expect good things to happen. We will give up on our dreams. Decide today that you are someone who is capable of learning how to get back to our original 'source'. Nobody knows more than the manufacturer how the computer is supposed to function. Restore your original factory settings. They are found right in the word of God, the Bible.

Our creator! Our manufacturer says these things about you: You are blessed. You are anointed. You are equipped. You are valuable. You are creative. You have the favor of God. You are all able to do what he calls you to do.

By now—you may feel like telling me that you don't feel like that, that you have a lot of problems. You may not feel that you are blessed but you need to start believing in God's blessings. Start talking about those blessings. Start acting in that manner, then God can make those blessings happen. This is what Faith is all about. Stop dwelling on negative lies and start believing in what God says about you.

Psalms say that all day long we should meditate on God's words. That means we should go around thinking: *I am blessed, I am valuable, and I am victorious.* What are we doing? We are programming our computer. The first thing we should do is set our mind in the right direction every morning. Just as you reboot your computer to get rid of the spam, so you should get up and declare that you will have a great day; that you are strong and ready for anything that comes your way.

The Bible says (Colossians 3:2):

> *'Set your minds on things above, not on earthly things.'*

If you do not set your mind at the start of the day, it is possible that the enemy will have an easier time reaching you with your usual or even new negative thought patterns. You do not have to dwell on any thought that comes into your mind; remember you can choose what you are going to think about. If the thought is negative and discouraging, you should immediately get rid of it and replace it with a positive Faith-filled thought.

If you are not disciplined in your thought life, you will never live a life of victory. When you dwell on a negative thought long enough, it gets hold of you and will keep you from accepting God's best gifts.

The words we speak are like seeds — they take root. We must water them by continually thinking about them and constantly dwelling in them. Just because somebody has said something negative about you, does not mean this thing is going to come to pass. All depends on what you do with the negative saying of people.

The one with the final say is — You. Nobody can keep you from your destiny except you. If someone (parent, teacher, friend, leader...) has spoken in a negative way about your life, do not allow those statements to take root by constantly dwelling on them.

Your earthly parents may not say positive things about you but your heavenly father says that He is proud of you; you can do all things through Christ; He says that your best day is not behind you...but instead, is still ahead of you. Decide today to live the life of someone who gets in agreement with God and start declaring the Word of God every day of your life. The dream that God has put in your heart, the seed of victory, of success and of hope may lie dormant year after year but you get to know that the seed is still alive. This dream is just waiting for someone to believe, to bring it to life. God does not let people say things to destroy your dreams. Do not let rejection and disappointment steal your sense of value. You are a child of the Almighty God.

Keep in your mind, it is not the things around you that will change you but it is your inner self that will make that change in your life. Remember! Man is a spirit and you have to control your life from your spirit. Do not let the outside control the inside but be controlled from within, and you will be richly rewarded. You can be delayed but you are not denied. You cannot change your yesterday but you can change your tomorrow.

Therefore, guard your mind. One way of guarding our minds is if we will spend time adding positive energy and statements into or way of thinking. Your mind is the birthplace, the incubator...the starting point of everything you do. Satan knows this. His entire strategy is to break your focus, sabotage your concentration and abort your assignment from God. So, the real battleground of life is your mind. Guard it well.

––––––––––––

'WE ARE TODAY THE SUM
TOTAL OF THOUGHTS AND
CHOICES MADE YESTERDAY.'

––––––––––––

CHAPTER 7

WHAT ARE YOU THINKING?

Whether you are rich or poor, man or woman, employee or employer, single or married, separated or divorced, teenager or adult, Christians or pagans, white or black, we all want to be better, we are driven by the dream to live better. God put something deep down inside us that evokes a desire to be more like Him. God didn't create us to be average and yet average is all too often accepted. Too many people settle for mediocrity in their thoughts, attitudes, or actions. It's time to put those negative mindsets away and rise higher.

Remember, God has put in you everything you need to live a victorious life. Now, it is up to you to draw God's plan out. We can't let wrong mindsets, a negative past, or other people's opinions discourage us or cause us to give up and quit pressing forward. People who want to live at their full potential have discovered that the good can often be the enemy of the best. As my spiritual father, Dr. Myles says: 'Your future is not ahead of you but it is trapped in you'. We must break the mental chain. Slavery is a mental conditioning. People can be free and still act like they are in bondage. This concept can be illustrated by a simple scenario.

A group of researchers performed a test on a dog. They tied a dog to a stake in open ground and threw him a piece of meat that was out of his reach. The dog dashed at the meat, but when he went toward this yummy treat, the chain yanked his neck. His neck was hurt. He jumped at it again, and once the chain yanked at his neck; the meat was just out of his reach. The researchers did this test for seven days. They would come out every day and put some food down. And each day he would run at the plate and hurt himself. On the eighth day, they released the chain and put the food in the same position. The dog did not move. There were no chains on the dog, yet the dog would just look at the plate. Even though they called, the dog would not move. They shouted, and the dog would not move. The researchers realized that if they did not do something, the dog would starve to death. This story illustrated anyone who has been oppressed for any length of time. Even when they are freed, they are scared. We have to break the attitude that we do not deserve success.

When you come to the understanding that God is your father, you will realize that the whole world is your property. The truth for me and the truth for you too is that there is no country that I should not have a right to enter because it is my father's property. There is no limitation to what I can achieve because my father owns everything. If you don't believe that then you will have the tendency of thinking like a slave. You take what is given to you rather than what you want. God says that He has given us His children the spirit that cries out 'Abba Father' (Gal 4:6). The scriptures reveal this truth: '*You are no longer slave, but a son; and since you are a son, God has made you also an heir. Formerly, when you did not know God, you were slaves to those who by nature are not gods*' (Gal 4:7–8).

Consider, the plural form 'gods'. We can be enslaved by many things that are not gods. The devil, the law, the government… none of these are gods. It is amazing how we can become so afraid of human institutions. God says, 'You were slaves to these 'so-called' gods'. These substitutes include the devil, the demonic powers, and people who have become consumed with negatives.

We worship so many people that are not gods. We worship them by nature. Nature refers to image. These things that we worship are not in the image of God. The devil and his lifestyle are not imprinted with God's image. The Bible goes on to say, '*But now that you know God — or rather are known by God — how is it that you are turning back to those weak and miserable principles* (Gal 4:9). You destroy principles by having principles. That is why we should know God's principles. The devil is referred to as the prince of darkness, and his demonic forces are called principalities. Many people think that the devil possesses people when in reality he possesses principles. He can brainwash you with principles that are lies about you. He has made you believe that you cannot accomplish what God has planned for you to do.

Now is the time for us to cast out thoughts that are killing us. The key to getting our minds in tune is a spirit. God says that he will give us His Spirit. The Spirit has to teach us how to call God father again. Religion has trained us to think that God is this great, big creature who is out to get us. We have to be retrained by the God kingdom's principles.

'GOD DOES NOT DEAL WITH
US ACCORDING TO OUR
FAITHFULNESS TOWARDS HIM,
BUT OUR FAITH IN HIM.'

CHAPTER 8

HAVING THE RIGHT IMAGE ON THE INSIDE

How you see yourself will determine what kind of life you are going to live. Too many people go around without any self-esteem and they have a poor self-image. That is because they do not understand who they really are.

We are born to win but society has a way of conditioning us to lose; through failure, through rejection, and through the mistakes we make. If we are not careful, the true image of what we really are will become distorted. You have the blood of a champion on the inside. God created you in His image. You did not come from any ordinary source. You came from the best of the best. God breathed his life into you. You have His royal blood flowing through your veins. He has equipped you with everything you need to succeed. You have the DNA of the almighty God.

The first step towards having a life of victory is to understand who you really are: a child of the highest God. Think about champion race horses. They are very small at birth but their owner is confident that they will be the best at winning races when they mature. That is the way you need to see yourself. You may have some weaknesses; you may not be the best looking, and you may not be the most talented or the most intelligent but you know that you come from a long line of winners. You may not see it now but in your DNA there is strength, ability, wisdom, courage, success…It does not matter what your present condition is, as that does not change your DNA, does not change what is in your blood. It was put in you by the creator of the universe.

Some people have believed these types of lies of the devil: *you are not good, you come from the wrong family*—but they need to go back and check their bloodline, the seed of the almighty God. Instead of focusing on your weaknesses, stop focusing on the mistakes you have made and start seeing yourself as God sees you. As far as God is concerned, He has already granted you the title of 'Champion'. You are predestined to be a winner, to overcome.

Ephesians 2:10 says that you are God's masterpiece. You need to start seeing yourself as forgiven, as a new creation…one who is strong, anointed, empowered, and full of possibilities. You are earmarked to do what God called you to do. People may have tried to put you down by telling you that you cannot make it, that you are not qualified…Remember that people cannot determine your destiny, but God does. Do not allow what other people have done to you to destroy the image of God inside you. One thing I have learned is that no one can make you feel inferior without your permission. How you feel is totally up to you whether you allow those words to take root and begin to disturb your self-image. You can either believe what others say about you or you can believe what God says about you.

A fifteen year-old boy was not doing very well in school and the teacher told him that he would probably never pass his exams and that he should begin to learn something different. This young man did not realize that God did not make him to be a failure, a quitter. For the next seventeen years, he just lived from day to day. He did any jobs that came his way. Every time he tried to make progress, the words of that teacher would come to him: *you are not talented; you do not have what it takes.* These false statements were allowed to take root. The picture that was painted in his mind was very disturbing. He did not see himself with the real image of God: a winner with God's DNA. Rather, he saw himself as unintelligent. One day something interesting happened. He applied to a company for a mundane job, but the company had a policy that every potential candidate should take a small intelligence test. When this young man took the test, he scored higher than anyone in that company's history. In fact, he qualified for a position at a senior level. He was extremely intelligent but for seventeen years he had allowed negative words to convince him that he was an average person. A light was switched on that day. This young man realized that he was not ordinary but that he was special. Oddly, he did not take that senior level position; instead he began to act like someone with authority and worth. He began to write books and even formed his own company. Everything changed when he realized what he really was.

Ephesians 1:3 says that God has equipped us with every spiritual blessing: *'Praise be to the God and Father of our Lord Jesus Christ, who has blessed us in the heavenly realms with every spiritual blessing in Christ.'*

Notice that it is in the past tense. This verse does not say that God is going to do it one day. This blessing is in you. It is inside you. If you are in agreement with God, your feelings will change. Do not let the opinions of other people create a stronghold in you.

Understand this principle: *'you already are whatever God has called you to be'*. If God says that a blue shirt is white, it is white even though it is blue. The shirt will change to white because God is not a man who can lie. To activate this blessing, you need to start believing it. Keep going back to check your spiritual birth certificate. Remind yourself who your heavenly father is. Recognize what God has given you. You are wonderfully made. Do not say negative things to yourself. Stop criticizing God's creation. One day Jesus said to the blind man, 'Become what you believe.' (Matthew 9:29). That is a powerful statement. We will become what we believe about ourselves. God wants you to make a mark in your generation. This mark can be created today. Start by reprogramming your thinking. Start seeing yourself as solid Gold from the inside.

Philippians 1:6 says that: *'He that began a good work in you will continue to perform it until it is completed.'* Jacob was a deceiver. He cheated his own brother. But God did not give up on Jacob, as He knew what he had put inside him. He changed his name to Israel. Where you are now is not where you are going to end up. In every Jacob, there is an Israel. In every Saul, there is an Apostle Paul.

Staying alive your whole life can come about with a great deal of enthusiasm. Too many people have lost their enthusiasm. At one time, they were excited about their future. They were pursuing their dreams. But along the way, they came across some road blocks. Things did not work out. They did not get the promotion they wanted. Their relationship failed. They suffered health problems. And they gave up. Maybe they are breathing but not really living. They are alive but they are not full of life. What happens is that they stop dreaming, they stop pursuing their goal. They have lost their purpose in life. If we are going to stay alive our whole life, we have to keep our dreams in front of us. We have to have a reason to get up each day. We need to know that we are people of destiny.

You did not accidentally show up on planet Earth, but God knew you before you were formed in your mother's womb. He has an assignment for you. There is something God wants you to accomplish. Somebody needs your love, your smile, your encouragement. The quicker you become convicted that you are created to make a difference, to impact on our society, to make the world a better place, the better your life will become.

Inside you right now there are dreams and desires put there by the creator of the universe but over time, life tries to destroy those dreams and desires. It starts little by little. A disappointment here, a set back there, a failed relationship...then all of a sudden, you get stuck in life. You cannot go further. Now, you are stuck in believing that the end is near. You cannot rise any higher. The problem here is that you are allowing life to take you over.

The Bible tells us the story of the man with the withered hand. I emphasize that the Bible does not tell us his name or his country. This man could talk and he had friends but his hand was withered. This meant he could not hold on to anything. Life was passing him by. What he used to aim for, what he used to be passionate about had faded. This unfortunate man, accepted his condition. He had an excuse: his hand was withered. When this man encountered Jesus, his life took on another meaning. Jesus did not comfort him. He did not say that he felt sorry for him. Jesus asked him to do something that before this very moment, he had been unable to do before. He said to him: 'stretch out your hand'. That means this man had to make a decision. He either had to take a step of faith and shake off his past failures, which his mind was telling him that he could not do, or he would instead choose to stand back and make excuses: 'I cannot do that, as my hand is withered. I have been in this situation too long.' He could have come out with all the excuses that would keep him in his infirmity, but this man believed that God could restore his hand; He could give him a new beginning. He stretched out his hand and he was instantly made whole. Look at the flowers that somebody gives you as a sign of love or as a thank you. After a couple of days, those flowers just wither. That is what happens in life. It starts out very strong, vibrant. You are excited about your dreams; you are passionate about your future. You start confronting dis-appointments; setbacks, failure and life slowly starts to break you down. Now you think that your dreams will never come to pass. You start developing the wrong mind set. Some people today are breathing but they are not living.

Life may try to change your destiny but God is telling you to stretch out your hand. Look to move to a new level. Look to do something that you could not do before. Take a new stance on life. Write a letter and in this letter, enlarge your vision. Get rid of any wrong mindset. Maybe your parents or your teach-ers raised you in the culture of believing you would never be successful. Do not believe those lies that come from the devil but stretch out for a higher level. Maybe your own thoughts are telling you that it will never get better. There could be a tug in your mind saying, I will never accomplish my dreams; just stretch out to the end. Get a new vision for your life. Stir up the dreams that God has put inside you. You may think that it is taking a long time or that you are getting too old but that dream is still alive. God is saying this is your year to do something that you never did before. This is your year to break free to the opportunities that are beyond your normal bounds.

God said in Isaiah 43:19:

> *'See, I am doing a new thing! Now it springs up;*
> *do you not perceive it? I am making a way in the*
> *desert and streams in the wasteland.'*

God wants to do something new in your life. You may try a thousand times and hit a brick wall but God is saying: 'do not fear. I am with you. I still have a plan for you and you are in the palm of my hand; if only you believe all things are possible.' When you give God praise it is as if you are watering a seed. Thank God that He is working behind the scenes, that he is arranging things in your favor. If you know that God has put something in your heart, even if you have to pursue it for the whole of your lifetime you should never stop trying. Keep believing. Set your mind in the right direction.

You will never leave where you are, until you decide where you would rather be. The day you make a decision about your life is the day your world will change. Move decisively towards the goals you have established. Intolerance of your present creates your future.

'DO NOT ACT ON WHAT YOU FEEL,
ACT ON WHAT YOU KNOW.'

CHAPTER 9

THE KINGDOM – THE POWER – THE GLORY

You are created with the mandate to extend the Kingdom of God on earth. And this Kingdom is the manifestation of the Power and the Glory of God.

The Bible tells us in Matthew 6:13 what Jesus said as prayer: '...for yours is the Kingdom and the Power and the Glory forever. Amen.'

We call it the Lord's Prayer. It was not the Lord's Prayer but a part of the prayer that He taught his disciples in order for them to pray and think this way. We call it the colonial Prayer in the Kingdom's teachings. The Bible talks about the Kingdom of God and The Kingdom of Heaven. What is the difference between them? First let us read 1 Chronicles 29:11:

> '*Yours, O LORD, is the greatness,*
> *The power and the glory,*
> *The victory and the majesty;*
> *For all that is in heaven and in earth is Yours;*
> *Yours is the kingdom, O LORD,*
> *And You are exalted as head over all.*'

Jesus picked this prayer from David. The Kingdom of Heaven is God's political structure for His kingdom to function on the Earth, even though it is called the Kingdom of Heaven. It is the Kingdom from Heaven brought to the Earth. The Kingdom of God includes the Heaven and the Earth. Man is God's political structure to influence the Earth. Our mandate is to extend the Kingdom of God on the Earth. Jesus is the Head of this political structure (the Kingdom of Heaven). According to the Bible, He is to rule on Earth. Every one of us is a member of this Kingdom. It is our responsibility to bring the Kingdom of Heaven to the Earth. We are trusted by God to do this. There are some Christians who have not accepted that responsibility. They belong to the Kingdom of God but are not functioning as citizens of the Kingdom of Heaven. You become a citizen of the Kingdom of God by being born again. But that does not mean that you are a full citizen of this Kingdom. On Earth your work for the Kingdom of Heaven should begin with evangelism, winning souls, because we must influence the Earth to accept God's Kingdom. This mandate is clearly defined in Psalm 145:9–13:

> *'The Lord is good to all, and His tender mercies are over all His works. All Your works shall praise You, O Lord, and Your saints shall bless You. They shall speak of the glory and shall praise You, O Lord, and Your saints shall bless You. They shall speak of the glory of Your kingdom and talk of Your power, to make known to the sons of men His mighty acts, and the glorious majesty of His Kingdom. Your Kingdom is an ever lasting Kingdom, and Your dominion endures through out all generations.'*

The Bible calls every believer a saint. Saints are not necessarily dead people upon whom religious leaders have bestowed the title. Paul wrote to the saints of Philippe, to the saints of Ephesus, as well as to the saints of Corinth. It is not the saints in Heaven who shall speak of the Kingdom. It is the responsibility of every believer to speak of the glory of the Kingdom of God and talk about His power to make known to the sons of men God's mighty acts.

The Hebrew word 'power', when translated, refers to mighty power. What is the glory? Some define glory as excellence, beauty, virtue, splendor, majesty. Others define glory as excess, the beauty of God's holiness. Glory is that which inspires or causes honor. When something happens that causes you to give honor, admiration and respect to someone, that thing has glory. What is causing Glory in the Kingdom of God? It is a Kingdom different from life on the Earth. This Kingdom is one where there is no sickness, no disease and no failure. It is a Kingdom where everyone is prosperous, and of equal worth. It is a nation with God's lifestyle. You have to understand that there is a difference between knowledge and Faith. David knew the difference between the Kingdom of God and the earthly kingdom. David knew the difference between what God is and what He does. The New Testament does not talk to us about Faith. All the teachings about the Kingdom of God after the resurrection do not teach about Faith. The NT does not try to get us to have Faith, but it is actually telling us that we have it. It tells us how to grow it and strengthen it. Every born again is impacted with a measure of Faith.

Romans 12:3 says that God gives to everyone a measure of Faith.

Faith is not a problem with many Christians. The problem is knowledge. Faith is based on promise, while knowledge is based on information. When David said: 'Who is the uncircumcised Philistine', he had knowledge of circumcision. He had knowledge of the implications and the benefits of circumcision. He knew the meaning of his circumcision. The word of God had already given to David that clear information that Israel would not fall before the uncircumcised. To David, it was not something about which he tried to have Faith but something that he already knew.

When you know something, you do not need to consciously get Faith. Your knowledge gives you Faith. We are talking here about the 'revelation knowledge'. It is not the knowledge that you get by reading something or by agreeing to something. We are talking about a special knowledge that has been accepted and has become applicable in life.

The difference between Joshua's generation and Moses' is that Moses' generation was a people who came out of Egypt. They continually asked Moses what God was going to do; it was asked how God would give them water and food because they were thirsty and hungry. These people needed to find this information through Faith. It was unnatural for water to come out of nowhere in the desert. Also, it was unnatural for food to come out of heaven. That was a miracle for them. They knew only how to work hard for the things they needed in life and now Moses was telling them about this kingdom. They were afraid of dying. They needed Faith to fight their preconceived ideas. That is why the Bible says that this generation could not enter the Promised Land, because they could not be persuaded out of their unbelief. But the Joshua generation had a different spirit. Here is the generation that grew up in the desert. They just saw the manna coming out of heaven. They did not pray. They just saw the manna coming down. They started their life as little children standing before the Red Sea and they watched how God divided the water, how the manna came from heaven. They did not know anything about Egypt. They did not know about the suffering of Egypt.

I would like to emphasize something here. A lot of people are in bondage because of the knowledge of their past. They have too much knowledge of suffering in the world. They are too familiar with this knowledge and it is difficult for them to believe in another better world. They are too familiar with Egypt. But the Joshua generation is different. They came to Jordan where Joshua did things differently. This generation looked at things differently. This generation did not have to express Faith. Faith was already in them. They knew what to do. These were the children of the covenant. The Joshua generation understood the meaning of circumcision.

In this kingdom that you and I become part of, we shall speak of the glory of God. The glory of this kingdom is a people without defeat; a people with excellent spirit. This spirit dwells in us; and will not produce excellence in us unless we let the process happen. You will not know what spirit you are made of until you put yourself to the test, until you act.

'WITHOUT A DEFINITE MAJOR PURPOSE, YOU ARE AS HELPLESS AS A SHIP WITHOUT A COMPASS.'

NAPOLEON HILL

Until you discover your gift and see how whatever gift God has given you is important in your life, you can only be an imitation. When you discover your gift, you find your arena of authority in this world. Authority is the inherent ability not only to execute your gift but also to do what you were born to do. When you discover who you are, and are able to live to the fullest with this gift, you can be authentic. The discovery of yourself makes you natural and an original, not a fabricated imitation. When you are natural and do what you were naturally created to do, your maintenance is low. If you try to do something you were not naturally born to do, then you will need a higher maintenance style life and you'll depend on artificial sustenance. The cost will be extreme. You will also spend most of your life on maintenance and not in service. Life becomes a struggle, a torture, and a burden. The creator wants you to be yourself and fulfill your purpose. When you do, the creator supplies everything you need.

When you discover who you are, you understand your value to the world and your importance to the human race. You recognize you have a contribution to make. You realize that your value does not come from the world. Rather, you give your value to the world. When you know who you are, you do not need to impress anyone. You do not have to prove anything to anybody. When you discover who you are, there is no one to compete with because you are an original. Other people's gifts or successes do not threaten you because you know that others can never replace or become you.

When you discover who you are, you become distinctive. You do not compare yourself to anyone else because you know there is no one like you. But people who are not sure who they are remain insecure and grasping. When you discover your authentic city, the jealousy in your life disappears. Being jealous of someone or someone else's circumstance or material items is only possible when you believe that someone can take away what you have, or that someone has something you do not have. Once you become a human being with confidence that is 'real' no one can take away your purpose and your gift. The Bible says that we are all God's workmanship created for good works in Christ (Ephesians 2:10); this means that we have all been created with different gifts to accomplish different and unique functions in the world. Your belief about and in yourself, based on who you are and what you have been given to do, cancels out the fear of others undermining you.

God wants you to be more blessed tomorrow than you are today. Your best days are not behind you. They are in front of you. Do not make little plans for your life. Do not have little dreams. Get rid of that defeated mindset. You are a child of the Most High God. God has breathed His life into you. He planted seeds of greatness in you. You have everything you need to fulfill your God-given destiny. God has already put in the talent, the creativity, the discipline, the courage, the wisdom and the determination. Everything you will ever need is all in you or within your reach. You are full of potential. But you have to do your part and start tapping into it. You have to make better use of the gifts and talents that God has given you.

Did you know that there is a reason for your existence? God knew you before you were even formed into a fetus. He has a specific plan for your life. Your job while you are here on earth is not to choose your destiny but to discover it. Many people search for fulfillment their entire lives and never find it because they fail to discover their purpose. God is the Creator of all things. Your life is not a mere coincidence or a mistake, but a part of His plan; He has a specific assignment for you. Do you know what it is? Are you ready to discover who you are? If not, here are 10 questions to help you discover your true destiny:

1.   What is your deepest desire?

Psalm 37:4 says:

> *'Delight yourself in the LORD and he will give*
> *you the desires of your heart.'*

When you decide to serve God, He will actually give you the desire to do what you were created to do. You will know it is a God-given desire because it will line up with His Word.

2.   What stirs your passion?

Passion is the zeal, enthusiasm, excitement and intensity you feel about things that are important to you. It will stir you to action. What bothers you the most? God may be calling on you to find a solution to a problem or to be a solution to a problem.

3.   What comes natural to you?

Have you ever taught someone how to do something that you could do with your eyes closed? It may have seemed simple to you, but complex to them. What is that natural talent or ability you have that others do not?

4.   Where do you get real results?

In Luke 13:6–9, Jesus gave us a time guideline for how long it should take to 'try something out,' such as a job, career, business or ministry. He gave an example of a man who had a fig tree in his vineyard and had been checking for three years to see if it was producing fruit. Then Jesus asked the question, 'Why cumber it the ground?' This was a nice way of asking, 'Why is this thing taking up space?' What is taking up space in your life?

5.   What is the witness of the Holy Spirit in your spirit?

God will confirm the plan He has for your life. He will sometimes speak through dreams and visions or in a still, small voice. He will make sure He gets the message to you in one way or another. Are you listening? To hear and recognize His voice clearly, you must position yourself by spending time seeking Him, diligently praying and studying His Word.

6.   What do mature Christians see in you?

Keep in mind that a 'mature Christian' is not just someone who has been saved for a while, but instead is a Believer who consistently makes decisions based on the Word of God. Mature

Christians can give you good advice about seeking God's will for your life.

7. What career or ministry that you can pursue with the peace of God?

Philippians 4:6–7 says to pray with thanksgiving and let your request be known to God, and He will bring you peace about the things that concern you. Let the peace of God in your spiritual self-guide you and confirm His will for your life.

8. What thoughts, visions or dreams are impossible to put out of your mind?

God speaks to us in various ways. He will give you thoughts, visions and dreams, but your job is to recognize when they are God's message and when they are not. You will know God has given you a dream, vision or concept when you have spent time seeking Him. He will confirm it through His Word, as well as through people who may speak in your life about the situation. In addition, you will see situations and circumstances line up to make your dream or vision come to pass.

9. What goal or ambition can you dedicate yourself to 100 percent, for the rest of your life?

Is there something you can do for hours and really enjoy? What career or job could you do for the rest of your life? When you discover your purpose, it will incorporate all of your gifts, talents and strengths, and you will have a passion for it that enables you to do it even when you are tired.

10. What do people volunteer to help you accomplish?

When you find what you were created to do, God will send people, opportunities and resources to help you along the way. Is there something you do that people want to support? When you get into that place, you will find total fulfillment. Don't waste another moment trying to find satisfaction in all the wrong places; find God's true purpose for your life today! Remember! Your situation or circumstance is not your destination.

This book is to help you live the life of God here on earth. The discovering of your true self is the key to God's kind of Life. Remember! We are all born the same way: dumbnaked-speechless. Kingdom blessings.

ENDNOTES

Dr. Myles E. Munroe, kingdom quotes.

Mike Murdock, seed of wisdom.